Psyching Up for Tennis

Psyching Up for Tennis

JACK LEEDY, M.D.

MORT MALKIN

Basic Books, Inc., Publishers   New York

Library of Congress Cataloging in Publication Data

Leedy, Jack J.
   Psyching up for tennis.

   1. Tennis—Psychological aspects. I. Malkin,
Mort, joint author. II. Title.
GV1002.9.P75L43   796.34'2019   76-43467
ISBN: 0-465-06518-X

FOR

Jill and Norma

CONTENTS

FOREWORD

In *Psyching Up for Tennis,* Drs. Leedy and Malkin have spelled out in great depth and with considerable humor the interrelationships between the mental and physical stresses and strains of the hackers and stars in their pursuit of excellence in what is, I think, the best of all games.

"Psyched up," according to the *Harper Dictionary of Contemporary Usage,* means "prepared mentally and emotionally." "Psyched out," on the other hand, means "disturbed mentally and emotionally."

In my forty-four years in tennis I have frequently been both psyched up and psyched out. I have experienced all of the emotions described by the authors: *Fear,* when in 1957 as captain of the U.S. Davis Cup Team, we were about to lose the Inter-Zone Final to Belgium, which would have meant an expense of $30,000 to the already poor United States Lawn Tennis Association. *Joy,* when we in fact won, which guaranteed a profit to the Tennis Association of $50,000. *Grief,* when at the age of fourteen, after dominating most of the match and feeling confident, my concentration waned and

I lost the City of Cincinnati Boys Finals. I can remember crying for what seemed like twenty-four hours and vowing never to play the game again. And more *grief* when it rained for the last three days of the U.S. Open Tennis Championships when I was Tournament Director. *Anger,* mostly at myself for committing errors of tactics and judgment, but especially when I was dropped from the U.S. Davis Cup Team because I would not play the game of tennis politics! Complete and utter *surprise,* when in 1957, without any forewarning, I was dismissed as Davis Cup captain after I had led our team to several Challenge Rounds with, in some years, very little talent. And finally *yearning* as a youngster to be better and better at the game I grew to love so much; *yearning* as a young circuit player to be the national champion (I came close in 1944 and 1945); and now as a "veteran" or "seasoned" player, *yearning* to see the game continue to grow and develop in an orderly and healthy fashion.

Psyching Up for Tennis explores these feelings and shows not only how they can adversely affect your game, but how they can be controlled to improve your play. This useful book also makes you aware of the various physical functions involved in each mental and physical act—whether planning your strategy or executing a perfect overhead smash. In short, it will keep your adrenalin flowing!

BILL TALBERT *

---

* Bill Talbert has won thirty-eight national championship titles in twenty-five years of amateur competition. He was captain of the winning United States Davis Cup Team in 1954, and served as tournament chairman and director of the U.S. Open Tennis Championships at Forest Hills from 1971–1975.

PREFACE

Most Americans have a burning desire to win. The trait is part of human nature, and in my world travels I have seen it wherever tennis is played. Spectators, too, like to be associated with winning. Everybody loves a winner.

Merely wanting to win, however, is not enough. Without adequate mental and physical preparation, desire is only wishful thinking.

When two adversaries are more or less equally matched, mental attitude and other psychological factors provide the difference between winning and losing. I have often seen a player of lesser ability use a positive mental attitude to beat a stronger opponent. At a given level of play, success or failure in competition depends on several factors: physical conditioning, desire, pride, and guts. All have psychological roots. Even physical conditioning develops from the determined pursuit of an objective.

There is another side to success. The final score of the match is the narrowest definition. Success is also the knowledge of having played up to one's own standard of proficiency. In this sense, success is a personal, emotional matter.

The psychological factors involved in tennis are many and varied, and must be developed to suit the individual player. *Psyching Up for Tennis* is a welcome help to players at all levels. Each player can use this volume to custom tailor the elements of psychology to individual success.

GARDNAR MULLOY *

* Gardnar Mulloy is a member of the Tennis Hall of Fame, and, with Tony Vincent, won the Senior Doubles Championship at Wimbledon in 1975.

ACKNOWLEDGMENTS

We wish to thank our many colleagues who gave generously of their time and knowledge. Through them we were able to gain insight into much of the current work relating to body and brain function. Especially helpful were Eugene Antelis, Robert Cornell, Robert Cupolsky, Vincent Fisher, Bernard Gutin, Gerald Imber, Leo Koven, W. T. Lieberson, Donald Michielli, Michael O'Leary, Gideon Panter, Norman Scherzer, Richard Stein, and Lenore Zohman.

We also wish to thank the many tennis players and other athletes who allowed us a glimpse of their thoughts and personal experiences. We spoke to players at all levels from novice to touring professional; particularly helpful were Natalie Bartner and Lilly Lowinger.

We are indebted to Sheldon Naftal, Susan Raboy, and our other research associates, who provided us with a wealth of materials on everything from tennis before the Renaissance to the transphosphorylation of phosphocreatine for the resynthesis of the high energy bonds of ATP.

A special tribute is offered to Murray Schneider, who has

been our ambassador to the tennis world and whose enthusiasm for this book has been as great as his enthusiasm for tennis.

Our deepest gratitude is extended to Herb Reich, Director of the Behavioral Sciences Program, Basic Books, Inc., whose suggestions during the development of the book have been invaluable; and to Patricia Osband for her outstanding editorial assistance.

Most of all a great hosanna for Jill Reintjes Malkin, our private editor, who has given of her days, weeks, patience, and fine literary judgment.

JACK LEEDY AND MORT MALKIN

Psyching Up for Tennis

INTRODUCTION

Why Tennis?

TENNIS appears to have violated the prime law of nature: that energy and matter can neither be created nor destroyed. In fact, the masses of tennis players seem as limitless as the energy they devote to the game. More people are playing and more people are watching the players play than ever before. As more interest is created in the game, more players materialize, and so the spiral rises.

The reasons for the attraction to tennis are many, varied, and interrelated. Tennis requires no team players. If "Anyone for tennis?" produces one other body, there is a game. Tennis requires minimal equipment, minimal amounts of time, and now it can be played year-round. Practically anyone can play, the basic rules and moves are relatively simple, and there are no age limitations.

For most sports, degree of participation and age are inversely proportional. Victory is to the quick and the strong. Thirty-five is the usual retirement age for professional athletes. At the recreational level, athletes bow out of most sports when they leave school, or shortly thereafter. The notable exceptions are tennis, golf, sailing, bowling, boccie, and fishing. In these, experience counts heavily, and patience and skill can outweigh the advantages of youth.

Recent years have seen increasing tennis activity among the over thirty-five set. The number of senior players has increased substantially. Many of those who played in their youth have either returned or never quit, and many new middle-years players have appeared. Masters tournaments for specific age groups continue to proliferate. Some of the former stars periodically recapture a bit of glory. Gonzales, Talbert, Mulloy, Seixas, McKay, Savitt, and Sedgman are just a sampling of the names on the senior scorecards. Although well past thirty-five, Ken Rosewall and Rod Laver are kept out of senior play because they are just too good. Others of us can look forward to a lifetime of tennis without worrying about getting run off the court by some fresh kid devoid of proper respect.

Tennis holds other attractions. It can be played by both men and women, large or small. In other sports, height and strength are critical. Imagine Arthur Ashe, at 145 pounds, as a hammer thrower or fullback. Imagine Ken Rosewall, at 5′8″, as a forward or even as a backcourt man in basketball. Moreover, tennis is faster, more complex, and more challenging than jogging, easier on the hands than handball, better exercise than bowling, and more socially competitive than golf.

Much has been conjectured recently concerning human tendencies toward possessiveness and aggression. Whether these traits are innate or not, they are certainly American. Perhaps that is why tennis has caught on here. Court behavior is aggressive. The serve, the advance to the net, the overhead smash, and even the drive from the baseline are all aggressive elements of the game. But tennis also has its defensive, possessive, "territorial" aspects. Each player "defends" his side of the court; the net can be considered a "territorial boundary" between the two players. Each time the ball is sent over the net, it can be seen as representing an "invasion." The lob and the drop shot are usually defensive or strategic maneuvers, the Trojan horses of tennis. At the end of the match, the victor ritually jumps the net into the territory of the vanquished. The racket may be considered the great equalizer, just as weapons have been throughout history. The tennis player who can use his racket to advantage can imagine himself a David slaying Goliath with his well-aimed strokes. Tennis thus presents the player with the opportunity to master, in microcosm, a very important aspect of American life—winning—through the individual, aggressive, competitive conquest of adversity in the form of a consciously depersonalized adversary.

Such a great variety of physical and mental attributes are needed in tennis that no one of them is critical. Speed, balance, general coordination, eye-hand coordination, reaction time, strength, endurance, and a tactical turn of mind all contribute to the making of a champion. A player who is not well endowed with one or more of the necessary qualities may compensate by special strength in others.

While it is true that practically anyone can play and that any player can compensate to some extent for physiological shortcomings, it is also true that not everyone can play to his or her satisfaction. There are few other games where the balance between the player's physiological and psychological attributes is so critical, or where the motives for playing and the interpersonal relationships between players can so directly affect the outcome of the game. The unity of mind and body has been experienced by almost all topflight athletes. This unity is probably more critical in tennis than in most other sports. Timing which is off by a hundredth of a second is the difference between just in and just out.

Emotional considerations rule behavior more than we like to believe, and tennis plays on the human psyche as few other sports do. All tennis players consciously try to play what they know to be their best game. But they seldom, if ever, reach their highest level of capability, and seldom feel that they have quite fulfilled their potential. The psychological makeup of the players has an important role in how matches are won and lost. The overall quality of the match may depend more on the emotional needs and interests of the players than on their combined and separate skills.

Psychology plays a greater role in tennis than in those sports, such as sprinting, where one competes against a combination of time and self—height, weight, age, skill, and inner standard of excellence—in order to attain an almost immediate goal. A singles match is a relatively drawn-out process by comparison and somewhat more than doubly complex since it involves competing against two self-set standards of excellence: the opponent's needs and skills as well as one's own.

There are almost as many approaches to psychology as there are people interested in it. One overall view sees the brain as guided by instincts, metabolism, culture, drives, and basic needs: man is a ship guided by the extrinsic forces of wind and tide. Another overall view holds that the brain absorbs experiences and then, after comparison, analysis, judgment, and decision, takes purposive action: man is the captain of his ship, free to set his own course. There is general agreement that both views possess a considerable degree of validity; and it is from this eclectic approach that the psychological factors pertinent to the game of tennis are presented here.

As important as psychology are the psychophysiological aspects of the game. The respiratory and cardiovascular systems are mainstays of endurance. The central nervous system and musculoskeletal systems determine coordination and balance. The endocrine glands influence metabolism and the response to stress. All these systems are in constant interaction with the psyche. There is no such thing in tennis as a "purely" physiological factor. An intricate interdependence exists between the physiological efficiency of brain-body function and the psychic efficiency of mind function.

That a change in the chemistry of the central nervous system can induce mental and physical alterations is common knowledge. We know the mental effects which can occur when alcohol, hallucinogens, tranquilizers, or stimulants work their ways on the brain. We also know that the muscle relaxant drugs prescribed for spasms do not act on the muscle tissue but act instead at various places in the nervous system, where they reduce the reflex impulse barrage to the knotted muscle. But it is less well known that, from a physical standpoint, the athlete in peak condition is on the border of exhaustion and, from a mental standpoint, his peak level of arousal is a step away from acute anxiety.

Three factors in well-played tennis are essentially psychological: motivation (the will to win), anxiety, and concentration. These factors are powerful though somewhat nebulous. To make matters worse, they overlap and interconnect. A fourth factor is essentially psychophysiological: the ability to make rapid adjustments. Few games involving so large a number of possible choices demand that decisions be made and enacted so rapidly. In less than a second, as the ball leaves the opponent's racket, the player must make several judgments as to just how the ball has been hit, and just how to counter the shot to his best advantage. The primarily psychophysiological element of precision—composed of perception, memory, learning, and the dynamics of decision making—is involved in such strategic considerations as the speed and true direction of the oncoming ball, where and how to return it, and where and how the opponent most probably will be readying himself for it. Fitness, a fifth and primarily physiological factor, is no less involved.

All these interrelated factors, involving muscle and brain, agility and speed, concentration and motivation, combine to form one all-important factor: situational creativity. This is the learned ability to make clever split-second decisions, involving unique combinations of moves, and to carry them through. Creativity is especially applicable to tennis because of the game's large array of strokes, placements, and possible combinations. It is not surprising that the personality traits generally associated with creative action—independence, skepticism, and high motivation—are invariably present in serious tennis players.

Why players lose and why men and women play so differently are questions influenced by primarily psychosocial factors. These include identity—the establishment of a unique self amid the brief and brutish anonymity of modern life— socialization and attitudes toward aggression. If psychological and psychophysiological factors tip the balance between two well-matched players, the psychosocial factors rig the scales before the game begins.

The many elements of tennis, in reality closely and persistently interrelated, are presented as apparently isolated entities solely for the sake of clarity. Just as no player can play an authentic game against a backboard and no mind can function well in prolonged isolation, so too no behavior pattern is devoid of stimulus or impact.

The succeeding chapters will teach no one the fundamental rules of tennis. Each chapter is geared to supply information to moderately experienced, conscientiously practicing players, from which they may gain insights as to why they now play as they do and, hopefully, how they can soon play to their greater satisfaction.

CHAPTER ONE

Motivation

MOTIVES are the reasons for behavior. They are the concepts, ideas, or psychophysiological states which incite the individual to action. Motives provide the "whys." Motivation is what sets the "whys" into action.

When asked why they play the game, most tennis players will almost immediately answer that the reason they play is to win. But few ask themselves what lies beneath their desire to attain this goal. Most of them would not have the slightest idea, anyway. The primary motives for most actions are not at the forefront of the average person's consciousness.

The importance of the role played by unconscious motivation in human activity has been recognized and accepted at least since the beginning of psychoanalytic investigation. Much of psychoanalytic theory is based on the concept that a person's behavior at any given moment is triggered and governed by drives, needs, desires, and previously learned patterns of response. No one can be more than partially aware of these stimuli.

The Motives

The recognized motive for most tennis played in this country is the players' desire to win. But why? What is the reason for winning?

Actually, winning is the means to two more important but less clearly recognized goals: recognition and, for the pros, money. And through the attainment of these goals comes the implied attainment of the primary, most important, but least clearly recognized goal: identity—the individual's sense of self.

Identity

What does "identity" mean? Shorn of mystique, simply stated, it means that everyone wants to be "somebody" and that no one really wants to die. As long as he is alive, each person wants to be actually aware—to "really feel"—that he is living, and wants a few others also to know it. And since corporeal death is inevitable, almost everyone wants to leave behind some bit of matter through which he or she can symbolically continue to exist. Hence such hostages to immortality as sports stadia, athletic endowments, various trophies for the most promising players, various halls of fame, and children.

These motives are fundamental, powerful, and pervasive; the fact that they can be stated simply does not make them any less so. Their ramifications cover the entire range of striving for power and status, from wars to beheadings, from bondage to bull markets, from batting in the most runs to baking the best cake, and from making the most sacrifices "for the sake of the children" to spray-painting one's name and street number on a subway car.

Identity, or a sense of self, need not come only from winning in competition. It can also result from engaging in noncompetitive sports, from exercise and the attainment of general "fitness." This is evident from a "before and after" investigation by A. H. Ismail and L. E. Trachtman of Purdue University. The researchers gave a group of middle-aged, sedentary men involved in a long-term exercise program an extensive battery of physiological and personality tests. By the end of the four-month program, those subjects whose fitness was poor at the beginning not only felt better but had begun to feel better about themselves, showing significant increases in self-sufficiency, emotional stability, and resoluteness. Personality change had accompanied physical change and the gratification of identity needs.

Recognition

Recognition is a powerful aid to the self in its constant striving to establish and maintain the all-important belief that it exists and is unique. The type and degree of recognition which winning at tennis can provide serves as ample reinforcement to this belief. Billie Jean King realizes that her constant striving to win is a part of the drive for identity which pervades many facets of her life. Pancho Segura, Jimmy Connors' coach, describes his protégé's intense motivation to win in this way: "He is a killer . . . he can't stand losing."

The degree of recognition which accrues to winning is stratified. The more powerful and prestigious the opponent, the more prestigious is one's victory over him. The absurd degree to which the identity-value of the win can become stratified is illustrated by a personal experience of a friend of ours, Marty Sher. Trained by his stepfather, a college tennis coach, Marty developed considerable ability and is a strong, consistent player. He never played professionally, never became known in tennis circles; none of the pros know him. On two separate occasions he played in a pickup match against a pro. Each time, as the match progressed and it became evident that Marty was going to take the measure of his opponent, the pro simply stopped, making some inadequate excuse as to why he could not continue. In each case, the pro could not tolerate the possibility of losing to an unknown.

Money

In this acquisitive society, one's worth in monetary terms is almost invariably equated with one's worth as a person. And since the way in which one is seen by others directly influences the way one sees oneself, it follows that the more money one has, the more recognition one will obtain, and the more steadfast will be one's feelings of self-worth.

Within the somewhat deeper context of psychoanalytic theory, money and other possessions are an extension of one's self. The terms "golden hand" and "golden arm" have direct psychological implications for the tennis professional. Loss of money can be seen as analogous to injury or loss of a part of the body. Some individuals will compensate for their fears of such loss by accumulating possessions.

The high income which accompanies winning in professional tennis is recognized by several of the pros as being less important in itself than in its function as a tool for the attainment and maintenance of identity. Billie Jean King recognizes that money is "the measuring stick by which people decide whether or not to appreciate you." And before his $100,000 match with Rod Laver, in February 1975, Jimmy Connors said, "The really important thing about the $100,000 is that it calls attention to the event. It draws the people and the television." He was much more concerned with the "chance to play the best and beat the best," and with the number of viewers in the television audience, than with the money per se.

While it goes without saying that a few hundred thousand dollars in yearly income is more of an attraction than mere travel expenses, there was a strong drive to stay on top in the days when tennis made its heroes no more than financially comfortable. In past years, it was the "winner" personality of the stars—Kramer, Gonzales, Sedgman, and Emerson, just to name a few—that made the game what it was.

The desire for the recognition which winning brings can motivate a player to intense bouts of concentration. Before 1974, for example, John Newcombe was anything but mediocre; yet he was still second best, sometimes to his countryman Rod Laver and sometimes to the notorious Rumanian, Ilie Nastase. Then, in late 1973, Newcombe made a commitment to tennis and to himself. He gave over all his waking hours (and probably not a few dreams, as well) to merging his being with tennis. As a result, he proceeded to trample everyone in sight. In the May 1974 finale of the World Championship Tennis matches, he ran through Okker, Smith, and Borg, just that easily. Newcombe himself recognized the psychological impetus behind his nine-month drive toward the championship: " . . . the real reason was recognition."

The Motivation

The motivation—the juice—which translates motive into action is *aggression*. More important than any racket, as important as all of the learned skills of the game, well-managed aggression is one of the tennis player's most powerful tools.

The trick is in its management. Like fire, aggression is a wonderful servant but a bad master. The most important tennis function of aggression is maintaining motivation. Too often, however, the player is ignited by negative aggression and his game becomes a heap of ashes. Sometimes the player so avidly blocks the use of aggression that his desire to win burns out and his game grows cold.

Aggression is a form of energy. It is psychophysiological in origin and usually surfaces as the result of frustration—the blocking of the satisfaction of one's basic drives and/or the blocking of the gratification of basic needs. Aggression is a means by which psychophysiological states of tension are resolved. Specifically, aggression is offensive energy; its implementation results in an offensive tool. In that characteristic lies the source of human fear of aggression, and much of its attendant mismanagement.

In the trees and in the caves, when confronted by a danger to security or life, if one could not flee one had to fight. Aggression is the juice of the fight, the energy for the kill. At this more constricted, better socialized time in human evolution, aggression has become the fuel of self-assertiveness. More importantly, aggression is the juice of creativity, of the mastery of skills, specific situations, and (in sum) of one's very life.

Of all the fires of the mind, humans generally find aggression to be the second most fascinating. Its existence within others is a threat, and its existence within themselves is both a threat and a fine excuse—but not one which they are inclined to allow others. The formula goes roughly like this: They are Evil, he is Rotten, I mean Well—but, I am only human.

Culture determines the general form in which aggression is expressed and the duration and intensity of its expression. The prevalent social attitudes toward aggression are all-important to the tennis player, for he will have been formed in part by them and will inevitably carry them into play. They can cause him to be crassly petty in placing shots at or near his male opponent's groin and his female opponent's chest. They can cause him to feel constricting fear and devastating guilt. If he is interested either in sportsmanship or in tennis for its own sake, they can be of little or no assistance.

Considerable pressure is placed upon the members of this society to control their aggressive tendencies. "Aggression" is popularly translated into a synonym for the negative manifestations of its use: hostility, anger, hate, and the application of brute force. Those many negative aspects which cannot be suppressed must be channeled into specifically acceptable activity, while the few positive aspects, though not suppressed, are not encouraged.

Cultural forces direct aggression in four ways in this society:

(1) Men are pressured to express their aggression in controlled form, and women are pressured to suppress their aggressive tendencies entirely.

(2) Aggression is channeled into competitive activity, and the individual is pressured to win.

(3) Our society is work-oriented, and the individual is pressured to win through work—and not necessarily through "an honest day's work for an honest day's pay."

(4) Ours is an "inside" society, and the individual is pressured to direct his aggression toward the "outsider"— the stranger, the rival, the opponent, or a member of the opposite sex.

If the individual does not accede to these pressures, he is pressured to fear reprisal and to feel demeaned: worthless, guilty, and unmasculine—a "loser." And since it is impossible to win at everything, everytime, one of the results of this pressure is a fluctuating sense of self-worth. One's sense of identity alternates between diminution and enhancement, requiring a reduction in the self-worth of others to satisfy its own need for growth.

Forms of Aggression

When directed toward the outside world, aggression is translated into words and actions.

Verbal Aggression

Although verbal aggression can also take the form of satire and sarcasm, most (and the most hostile) verbal aggression consists of profanity: figures of speech primarily pertaining to misalliances and misfortunes in such elementary spheres of activity as excretion, copulation, and motherhood. Since the imagination of the user of profanity is often rather limited, the content of verbal aggression tends to be repetitious.

Aggression can only be verbalized as other words are: whispered, sung, spoken in a "normal" tone of voice, shouted, or screamed. Since there is too great a tendency among humans to shout and too little to whisper, and since so few people think they can sing, the mode of delivery also tends to be repetitious. There are not too many great and creative profanity coaches around. Verbal aggression is easy to use, but most people find that it affords them sufficient satisfaction on no more than a sporadic basis.

Physical Aggression

The most hostile form of physical aggression is murder, a ritualized and restricted activity which, under ordinary circumstances, is the province of the few. Play and sports translate aggressive energy into socially acceptable action for the many. Play and sports are regarded in this society as second only to work as a universal form of human activity.

For the average person, tennis singles is the most directly combative physical sport available. The rules of handball and squash allow the player to hit the ball only indirectly toward an opponent—off the wall. Boxing is more individually combative, but the physical liabilities involved make it unattractive to the average person. In fencing, the mask and garb clothe the opponent in anonymity. A few centuries ago, there was a sport comparable to tennis in directly combative competitiveness, but now jousting has been relegated to motion picture extravaganzas.

Robert Ardrey characterized the space race, the Olympic games, and all other sporting competition as prime examples of the ritualization of aggressive tendencies, of channeling them into controlled, sanctioned modes of expression. We need only look to tennis for the substantiation of Ardrey's suggestion, for contrary to superficial appearances, tennis is not all gentility and politeness. Although it is a game of precise rules, with many elements of honor, aggression is evident in the strokes, the rush to the net, and even in the facial expressions of the players. The hitting of the tennis ball is so patently an outlet for normally suppressed aggression that the players themselves generally recognize it as such. In putting away a point, even the professionals will hit the ball considerably harder than is necessary, and such vehement shots are not always directed toward an undefended corner of the opponent's court.

Competition

In this society, the behavioral mode used most frequent to express aggression is competition. Tennis affords the player a vehicle by which to engage in face-to-face competition. In this, it is unlike such other popular sports as golf, track and field, swimming, diving, ice skating, archery, and marksmanship. In all of these the individual competes as much against himself as against his opponents.

The competitiveness inherent in sports like tennis does not build character, lead to happiness, or foster love; and contrary to the tenets of sportsmanship, it does not always tend to bring out the best in one. Increasingly, the emphasis on winning implements hostile rather than creative forms of aggression; more and more, how one plays the game becomes less and less important.

A rather delicate balance exists between sport as a safety valve, or sublimation, and sport as a reinforcement of negative aggression. In many instances, aggressive, competitive sports —of which tennis is one—increase aggression in the already hostile individual. Many sportswriters and critics have recognized that in intercollegiate athletics in the United States the many positive effects of competitive sports are outweighed by the negative ones. Intrinsic and extrinsic pressures to win are the prime negative factors. Exploitation of athletes, the breaking of rules, and a disregard of ethics have all resulted from the desire to win at any cost. Much of the pressure to win begins in Little League sports. When free to engage in unstructured and unsupervised play, kids find joy in sports. Too often, however, Little League sports have provided an outlet for the competitive needs of parents, at the expense of their children.

Of course, not all the Number One tigers are kicking up grass and clay. Competitiveness extends to work as well. In their steel and concrete cells, corporate captains of finance and industry are often at work before dawn. In the evening, on weekends, and on their infrequent vacations, their ever-present briefcases might as well be handcuffed to them. They live their lives reaching for the top rung. When this type of individual does achieve some measure of success, he often finds it impossible to stop what has by then become for him a joyless, compulsive activity.

Play

A generalized learning process in childhood, play is equally necessary for adults both as a diversion from the "real" life of work and as a ritualized means by which both positive and negative aggression can be expressed. Unlike work, play can be a nonserious activity initiated and stopped at the wish of the individual. Play is an interlude. It can produce pleasure, even euphoria, at minimal personal risk.

The concept of adult play includes most diversionary activities, a fact which common usage makes clear. We *play* chess, backgammon, and cards. We *play* roulette and the horses. We *play* tennis and other ball games. We *play* musical instruments. We construct *plays* on words. We *play* house. We *play* at being grown up. We *play* at life. We *play* at love. We *play* around.

In one sport, at least, play is pure and unencumbered. Kayak paddlers speak of freely playing in the rapids. And they do just that. There is no competition, just fun. Would that this were so in other adult games.

As everyday life increases in complexity, the necessity to escape, at least temporarily, from its worry, tedium, and pain also increases. Most psychotherapists now realize that escape is not always undesirable. The issue is how escape is achieved. Tennis provides a form of escape which is not just acceptable but respectable. It provides a respite from the daily occupational routine. The courts provide a different physical environment. The high degree of concentration necessary for effective play screens out all other environmental stimuli and negates, for a time, the usual concerns of everyday life.

As a vehicle of escape from internal and external stress, tennis has some parallels with alcohol, marijuana, and opium. Nevertheless, although some players experience a "high" from the game, tennis never involves a total separation from reality, as is frequently the case with drugs.

The normal work routine of most individuals requires mental rather than physical activity. For these individuals, exercise can function as a form of play, a diversion from their sedentary routine. Researchers attempting to explore the effects of exercise deprivation on individuals who regularly included exercise in their daily routine found that, despite generous financial offers, it was difficult to find subjects for the study. Most of the prospective subjects contended that regular exercise was more important than the money they were offered for participation.

In recent years, there has been a noted increase in physical activity as play, particularly in those sports, such as tennis, in which participation requires intervals of an hour or less. Many working people are forgoing lunch for the exhilaration of physical activity. In every case, the basic requirement of the activity is that it free the mind from the constraints of work.

Physical activity not only provides diversion, it can also be joyful, vitalizing, and highly sensuous. On a good day, the sprinter experiences the soaring, gliding, utterly unrestrained sensations of flying which skydivers and kite gliders feel every time. Like a dancer, the skater and skier can lose themselves in the rhythm of their bodies. Swimmers become enamored of the many-fingered caress of the water, and scuba divers can be lured by it to flirt with rapture of the deep. There is the exhilaration of riding at full gallop, of holding course with one's boat planing at eighteen knots, of belly-whopping down a snow-covered hill. At times, tennis players can be ballet-like in their motion. In a photo of Chris Evert taken in 1973, we know she is playing tennis only because she has a racket in her hand.

Tennis can bring with it the euphoria of those days when every shot turns to gold. The pros tell us of the days when their timing is perfect and their eye is "on," when everything comes together and their control is so perfect that they can put away winners with the precision of a marksman. When it happens, they don't want to stop playing, don't want to lose that cloud-nine feeling. These are the times when love of the game takes precedence over winning.

The nonpro can experience his share of joy, too. He may feel a lesser elation, have fewer "on" days and less perfect control. But for him there is still the "high" from an extended volley, and from the sound of the racket, and from the flight of the ball when a shot is hit just right.

Motivation

Why Players Play

Few people play tennis solely for the fun of it. Few play solely for exercise. Some play for recreational diversion. Of these, some play for the stimulation which this diversion provides.

Eli Wallach is one of these. He carries his racket and sneakers with him in all his travels, playing tennis in Hollywood, New York, London, and Rome. He finds tennis to be both a physical and a mental stimulant. After an hour's tennis, his blood is circulating well and he feels refreshed. He will often play at noon when he is to appear on stage in the evening. After a performance, however, he cannot take to the courts; then he must depressurize and relax. Tennis does not perform this function for him.

Eli offers some very interesting parallels between his tennis play and his profession. Just as athletes do, actors warm up before a performance. Eli arrives at the theater or studio a half hour beforehand; in this setting, he mentally reviews how he will handle specific lines, and tries to visualize himself on the set.

Eli wishes he could play tennis the way he acts: not only in terms of how well, but also in terms of method. As an actor, he seldom thinks of directions or cues during the performance. The acting just comes forth. His voice and physical being are merely vehicles for the acting. He becomes the character he is portraying.

But his tennis is nothing like that. His cerebral cortex constantly fires silent verbal directions at him: "Get your racket *back*." "Bend from the knees. Further!" "Watch the ball!" His actor's mind, however, does allow him some amount of illusion. He sometimes visualizes himself on Wimbledon's center court before a packed gallery; and if he hits a solid return, the illusion remains. But if he misses the shot, the image clicks off.

Eli wishes that his tennis just played itself. After all, he

Chris Evert exhibits grace on the court.

has been rehearsing for years and years now. His game is primarily defensive, but he has a strong point: the ability to disguise the direction of his shots. Many times, he deceives even himself.

Others who play for recreational diversion find that they can utilize tennis both as a tranquilizer and as a stimulant. Han Joo Kim is a radiologist who spends his 9-to-5 in a physical environment which is unlike that of most people. The X-ray department where he works is in the basement of a large teaching hospital. There is not a window in the entire place. In addition, all visual stimuli are in black and white. The uniforms of the personnel are white, the X rays are black, white, and gray. The work is sedentary, providing little physical stimulation.

After five days of stillness, Dr. Kim needs the exhilaration of a physical activity which makes use of all parts of the body. He craves sunlight and the natural spectrum. The Saturday and Sunday sun, sky, grass, and trees exert a magnetic attraction. Dr. Kim tried golf and jogging, but found the former insufficiently strenuous and the latter too dull.

If he has had an unusual amount of frustration and irritation at work, tennis also acts as a tranquilizer. It offers him relief from anger and anxiety. "I feel better after hitting a few hard ones," he says. While playing tennis, he is completely divorced from his work. Although his medical training has given him an extensive knowledge of anatomy, physiology, and biomechanics, he does not think in those terms while on the court.

His style of play and court behavior are a direct reflection of his personality. He is a young, slim man who is soft-spoken, self-assured, and in complete control of his emotions. On the courts he plays a strong but controlled game. If he tries to smash the ball the shot usually goes out. If another player throws a tantrum or indulges in gamesmanship, Dr. Kim becomes upset and loses his concentration. He will not play with that individual again.

There are also a few players whose primary motivation is self-challenge: the satisfaction of approaching their potential. And there are some who find it difficult to separate their vocational and economic affairs from tennis. One corporation president, Murray Schneider, considers tennis as a calling card. He takes his racket along on every business trip. His secretary arranges court reservations in the cities he visits, as unfailingly as she arranges his airline tickets. Murray feels that tennis enhances business rapport. Since 1970 he has found more and more tennis partners among the business executives with whom he deals. Since 1970, too, his own business has expanded. Which was cause and which was effect? In Murray's view the two were symbiotic. In fact, tennis fever is epidemic in the business community. So many corporations in Manhat-

tan have switched from restaurant lunches to court confer-
ences that daytime tennis reservations must be made weeks in
advance.

Because tennis is a game, it appears to be outside the constraints of life as it is really lived. Hence, challenge and defeat can be used by the player as vehicles for the expression
of hostility toward an individual who is unassailable within
the confines of everyday work or the general social structure.
This ploy is especially popular in the junior executive ranks
of business. Here, tennis becomes an instrument of focused
competition aimed at the establishment of a specific (ideally,
isolated) dominance over a particular individual in the same
business organization.

Such players will go to the extreme of spending a vacation
at one of the drill-intensive tennis camps, in order to sharpen
those particular strokes which will be most effective in dealing
with the individual to be beaten. Vic Braden's Tennis College
in California and John Gardiner's Tennis Ranch in Arizona
—each more like a chain gang than a resort—unwittingly pre-
pare a disproportionately large number of such warriors for
battle. The training includes not only strokes but strategy
and psychology as well.

Put to this use, tennis is as often a signal that the player is
a strategic pushover as it is a symbolic club with which to beat
up the enemy. Although such warriors are invariably straightforward as to their overt aim of winning, the role of unconscious motivation can be a devious one, on the tennis court as
at the office.

Motivational conflicts aside, the great majority of tennis
players do play to win. The importance of winning is evident
on all levels of tennis, from world class professional to weekend
hacker. For this majority, winning is a source of ego fulfillment. Tennis serves as a vehicle by which to win and thereby
enhance all-important feelings of adequacy and self-worth—
in effect, identity.

Motivation

Unfortunately, the element of play in tennis is becoming less and less significant. The game is becoming an increasingly ritualized activity, and is more and more being utilized as a means to an end—just one more work tool forged to establish business contacts, attain self-aggrandizement, and bring down others.

Hustling is not the exclusive preserve of Bobby Riggs. It has become fairly commonplace for players of even weekend ability to place bets on their game. A match won is thought doubly to certify self-worth. In the process, the possibility of self-actualization is negated. The individual's identity, the establishment of which is the primary motive for playing, grows alienated from its objective and becomes distorted. It grows smaller, meaner, and less and less meaningful.

When tennis becomes a catalyst for destructive tendencies, it is time to return the game to the status of play. To hear the swock of the ball hitting the "sweet spot" on the strings and to see the ball raising chalk dust on the base line can bring about euphoria. An extended volley can evoke a crescendo of exhilaration that rises with every return. It can even effect a spirit of oneness with an opponent. The only prerequisite is to be receptive, to enjoy the game as a game.

Then, playing up to one's potential is first-rate therapy for ego strengthening. Tennis, after all, can be fun.

CHAPTER TWO

Anxiety

THERE are many levels of consciousness, ranging from being asleep to being psyched-out, which can itself resemble a form of sleep. In sports, anxiety is synonymous with being psyched-out. Skillful tennis depends on the suppression of anxiety, the avoidance of being psyched-out.

The roots of anxiety lie partially in insecurity. The roots of insecurity lie in lack of preparation and inadequate motivation.

There is nothing intrinsically bad about anxiety. As with aggression, it is the negative aspects which are stressed in popular thought. Anxiety is, in fact, an absolute necessity. No exploration of the environment, no learning, no step toward self-actualization can take place unless accompanied by anxiety. One does not learn because one wants to; one learns because one *has* to, in order to stop feeling uncomfortable about being inadequate to handle some situation which one wants (is motivated) to be able to manage. That diffuse feeling of being very "nervous," tense, or uncomfortable "edgy" is anxiety. Aggressive acts, either creative or hostile, can alleviate anxiety. Which type of act works best in which type of situation depends to a great extent upon the individual's personality.

Too much anxiety can be destructive. There is a point in the course of learning and in actual tennis play at which anxiety is a distinct aid; beyond that, however, anxiety becomes first a hindrance and then a fatal impediment to learning and good play.

Becoming Aroused

One comes from sleep into a waking state. There are many levels of being awake, ranging roughly from being barely conscious, with one's awareness rather diffuse and one's perceptions rather misty, to being psyched-out, with one's awareness again rather diffuse and one's perceptions quite scattered. Most tennis involves three stages of awakeness which, for purposes of convenience, can be designated in this manner: at stage 1, the player is *aware;* at stage 2, the player is *aroused*; and at stage 3, he is *anxious.*

Some of the player's best concentration will take place at stage 1. When the player is nervous before a match, he is usually at stage 2. When he starts to fall apart at the prospect of an upcoming tournament or becomes so uptight that his arm has trouble swinging during the match, he is either at or approaching stage 3.

Like most vigorous physical activity, tennis requires a heightened degree of arousal. Tracking accuracy, strength of motion, and quickness of decision require an acute attentiveness. Until the player is so skilled that almost all play is "automatic," stage 2—where he is more than awake and less than truly anxious—is his optimum level of tennis consciousness. It is when he is aroused—highly motivated and only somewhat anxious—that the player learns best. And at those many times when his concentration is not total, stage 2 is also where he plays best.

Each stage of consciousness has many levels; the gradations are very fine, and one's level of consciousness is in constant fluctuation. One's mind and psychophysiological responses do not merely "step up" from being anxious or "step down" from being aware to being aroused.

Levels of Arousal

The tennis player must keep his degree of arousal as fixed as possible within a narrow range, the optimal stage of consciousness for the majority of tennis activity—that is, stage 2. If his arousal level becomes too low, there will be a lessening of motivation; if it becomes too high, he will begin to tighten up or "choke."

The arousal level making for maximum performance differs from one type of activity to another, from individual to individual within the same activity, and, for the same individual, from situation to situation within the same activity. Activities requiring fine motor coordination have a lower optimal level of arousal than do those involving the use of large groups of muscles. Sprinting and weight lifting require a higher level of arousal for greater efficiency of performance than does tennis.

Jimmy Connors is an example of a player whose entire being can change from one situation to another. Here is focused motivation at work. During tournament play, Connors throws his body into every shot; he dives after the ball when he cannot quite reach it otherwise; he is on the offensive at every opportunity, and then some. His coach, Pancho Segura, says that Jimmy can concentrate totally for two hours straight. Few others can come close to that. In contrast to his tournament

Jimmy Connors stretches for a high one.

play, Connors in practice looks like a strong, steady player, but hardly one of the best in the world.

These different levels of arousal have a neurophysiological and psychophysiological basis. The discovery about twenty-five years ago that electrical stimulation of a particular region of a cat's brainstem—the reticular formation—produced an awake, alert state initiated disciplined investigations of the neurophysiology of sleep and wakefulness. It was subsequently discovered that stimulation of the reticular formation of awake animals improved both their accuracy and reaction time in task performance.

It was subsequently found that the thalamus, hypothalamus, cerebral cortex, and several other brain centers also normally influence the waking state; that wakefulness is regulated by a series of rheostats with automatic feedback control mechanisms located throughout the brain; and that there are direct nerve fiber connections between the cerebral cortex and the reticular formation. As a practical matter, if we wish to produce alertness or drowsiness, we must rely on stimulating or depressing the cerebral cortex.

Altering Levels of Arousal

The nature of a stimulus, the degree of the player's psychological involvement with it or with the situation in which it occurs, a change from one type of stimulus to another, and a change in the intensity of the same stimulus can all directly influence the degree to which he is "awake" and alert. The substrate upon which the extrinsic stimuli act is not immutable. Arousal levels are heightened during certain times of the day, month, and year. Metabolic cycles, hormonal levels, and inconstant brain chemistry can yield different responses to the identical stimulus at different times. Most of us have had the experience of being upset over some minor matter at one time and not giving it a second thought at another.

Causes of Anxiety

Although the underlying causes of anxiety are numerous and often difficult to pin down, one major contributon can be found in the dissonance between satisfaction of basic drives and needs and the socially sanctioned methods and specific degrees to which these are allowed to be satisfied. Anxiety can result from a real or perceived inability to adapt to the environment as represented by physical challenge (such as threat of force by another individual), by emotional and social factors (such as a sudden change in human relationships), or by other factors. The environment may be only somewhat stressful, and not actually overwhelming. But if the individual is psychologically unprepared and/or the body's physical and physiological mechanisms are in a weakened state, anxiety can still result.

Such factors as physical injury, disease, and fatigue can also reduce the individual's capacity to adapt. Other, more subtle factors which can give rise to anxiety include two which are especially prevalent during the actual playing of tennis: inadequate preparation for particular situations and drastic changes in the environment. Playing in an important tournament, playing against a nationally known opponent, playing before spectators, or even playing on a strange court can raise arousal levels to the point where anxiety is detrimental to performance, where muscles are in partial spasm and muscle groups do not coordinate.

There are also strong cross-cultural and intracultural differences in the degree to which anxiety is experienced. For instance, it could be hypothesized that, within this culture, celibate priests experience less anxiety concerning impotence than do libertines!

Heightened anxiety is not limited to hackers, or even to strong club players. The world-class touring professionals are susceptible, too. Some of them describe it as "too much concentrated energy of mind." Others call it "choking."

Inhibition in tennis is commonly caused by anxiety. Beyond the generalized anxiety which usually accompanies tournament play, there is the specifically focused anxiety that surfaces when one plays an opponent known, say, for a big serve or great all-around ability. Chris Evert, ranked number one in the world in 1975 and 1976, is still tense and nervous when she plays Evonne Goolagong, the greatest natural talent among the women pros, and always unpredictable.

The greater the degree of recognition and identity enhancement which winning will bring, the greater the degree of anxiety which the player is likely to experience. After having lost to John Newcombe in 1973 Davis Cup play, Stan Smith said that he had been nervous at the start of the match, adding, "When you're playing Davis Cup, you're not playing for yourself. You're playing for your country; and it's an added pressure."

Personal animosity between opponents can result in heightened anxiety. For example, an unusual circumstance in the 1975 Wimbledon finals probably worked on the psyche of brash Jimmy Connors, who usually plays best in a virtual rage. Only two weeks before, Connors had announced a $5 million libel suit against Arthur Ashe, who had taken him to task for not playing on the U.S. Davis Cup team. At Wimbledon, Ashe did not even allow Connors the luxury of psychological repression of the affair. In silent calculation, he took to the court wearing a blue warmup jacket emblazoned with a red "U.S.A." During the match, he played a brilliant tactical game and quickly won the first two sets, 6–1, 6–1.

Connors displayed a rarely seen anxiety. His facial expression betrayed it, and so did his response to a heckler. Immediately after he failed to go after a cross-court volley, a voice called from the stands, "C'mon, Connors!"—implying that Connors was not playing up to championship caliber. Instead of his usual reply, which is to point to the sky with his middle finger, Connors turned and said, "I'm trying, for crissake."

Even when no personal animosities are involved, playing on Wimbledon's center court has the effect of substantially heightening anxiety. Two of the best women players, Virginia Wade and Billie Jean King, illustrate opposite reactions. Virginia Wade is emotional and demonstrative on court. The crowds respond to her wherever she plays, and in her native England she is a favorite. Her victory at Wimbledon this year was especially meaningful, since she does not perform well in the grip of heightened anxiety, and had never won a Wimbledon singles title before. By contrast, Billie Jean King performs there at peak efficiency. Her play rises to the occasion of what is, for her, the most important of all the tournaments.

For the recreational player, anxiety takes the form of tightness on a particular stroke or strokes. It is the all too common "choking"—the failure to have a smooth, free swing and natural follow-through. The service, overhead, and backhand drive are the most usual troublemakers.

Although there are many psychological factors contributing to the anxious state, improvement in two physical dimensions—strength and skill—will effectively diminish choking. Strength involves exercising the major muscle groups on the racket side of the upper body. The major muscles of the chest, back, shoulder, and arm are the crucial ones. They can be strengthened by playing plenty of tennis, but even more by weight work and isometric exercises. Skill involves tracking, coordination, and timing. It is best improved by drilling and to some extent by visualization techniques (mental practice).

It is no surprise that when skill and power improve, many of the psychological underpinnings of anxiety vanish.

CHAPTER THREE

Concentration

CONCENTRATION is the focusing of goal-oriented need plus goal-oriented work: a combination of intensified motivation and intensified effort bent specifically and exclusively toward the achievement of a specific goal. The specific goal of most tennis players is to win.

There is no disputing the fact that a world-caliber player can get out of a sickbed or stagger onto the court after an all-night orgy and beat a weekend player in straight sets. But why is it that Arthur Ashe can take the Wimbledon title early in July and barely make a respectable showing in the *Washington Star* tournament in late July? And why are the Australian players Court, Rosewall, Laver, and Goolagong all so dangerous when they are down a few games? And why are we hackers, who rally so well when we're warming up, struck by alternating attacks of rigor mortis and the flobbles when the match really starts?

Much more is involved than skill. It is the manner in which that skill is concentrated: the degree to which the player is motivated to win, plus the degree to which use of the necessary skills is focused toward winning, plus the degree to which this focus is maintained.

This is almost as difficult as it sounds—which is a major reason why we are hackers and they are pros. Every top athlete knows that winning a championship requires at least 95 percent motivational drive, concentration, and hard work. And, to these individuals, it is worth it.

Focusing

Concentration is three-phased. First, one must attain a state of readiness. Second, one must be able to focus. And third, one must be able to resist distraction, i.e., sustain focus.

Motivational readiness

This first phase is the process of getting psyched-up, elevating the attainment of a specific goal—in this case, winning—from a wish to a desire, and from a desire to an absolute necessity. In terms of tennis-psych, it means generating an unswerving need to win, working up the sure and certain knowledge that for the length of time it takes to do so, and regardless of the effort involved (real effort, that is, and not gamesmanship), beating that body on the other side of the net is literally all there is to life.

Here is where consciousness must be elevated to near-anxiety —almost to stage 2.5.

Focused motivation

This second phase is the all-important background element both in the warmup period and during the game itself. Every move and every combination of moves has one overall, all-important, ultimate purpose: winning the game. Winning must be the one and only "real" thing in the player's mind.

The higher the degree of motivation to achieve a goal, the easier it is to focus on achieving it. Formal investigations of the ability to maintain an intense degree of focused concentration (trance capacity) indicate that intense motivation invariably results in an increased degree of concentration. Practically everyone has heard of some incident involving an individual who, under extreme emotional conditions, has performed some extraordinary physical feat, like lifting the front end of a car to free a trapped child. And practically everyone has also heard that, under hypnosis, extraordinary feats of strength and endurance become commonplace.

Sustaining Focus

In this third phase, attention must be made to drop down toward stage 1—that is, by whatever means will work for the individual, anxiety must be reduced. Highly motivated concentration can do it by blocking out distraction: the individual makes himself aware of one goal only.

Intensifying the desire to win is not a difficult task for most highly motivated individuals. Since their need to achieve is rather high to begin with, their motivation to win can quickly be brought to a state of readiness. But focusing it tends to be more difficult for this type of personality, and maintaining focus is even more difficult.

Such people tend to become over-motivated, and hence distracted. They get so involved in why they have to win, in the planning of strategy and combinations of moves which they intend to use to achieve this goal, in all the reasons why the opponent deserves to be beaten, and in all the bleaker basics of competitiveness (which may or may not have much direct bearing on the specific game at hand) that they are unable to maintain the other necessity for winning—focused effort. They tighten up, they choke, and with everything going for them except sustained focus, they play a shamefully poor game.

Coping with Motivational Distraction

The pros have two principal ways of dealing with the detrimentally high degree of anxiety which is directly responsible for motivational distraction. These are (1) "staying loose," which serves to diminish anxiety and is both a pregame and an in-game tactic, and (2) when concentration wanes in-game, "focusing beyond," which is a method of heightening anxiety.

Staying Loose

Staying loose is, as Arthur Ashe says, trying not to try too hard.

Carole Caldwell Graebner tells us that the top pros have a rule of thumb to prevent choking: "Don't think, just hit." This philosophy is embraced by two major advocates of yoga tennis, Rick Champion and Timothy Gallwey. Each plays tennis with a oneness of body and spirit, but "out of the mind." A few of the top world-class players have shown a quiet interest in yoga tennis. Commenting on her 1975 Wimbledon victory, Billie Jean King used Zen terminology: "This is probably the closest I've ever come to a perfect match. I played out of my brain, and I don't think Evonne knew what hit her."

The proponents of yoga tennis contend that the mind is full of inner distractions and that, in order to keep it from interfering with the shot, it must be kept occupied. One suggested way is to concentrate on the ball and the pattern of the seams. There is no question that intense concentration on a single sensory source or motor activity can inhibit extraneous cerebral activity. For example, the breathing exercises taught in preparation for natural childbirth can block or at least diminish awareness of uterine contractions and attendant perception of pain.

Focusing Beyond

It is difficult to maintain the same high level of motivation for an entire match. There are many players who begin slowly, often losing a few games or even a set before playing up to capacity. Realizing that one might have to experience the known consequences of losing provides an excellent stimulus for the sharpening of motivational focus.

Focusing beyond the game to its possible negative consequences is a technique often used to advantage by achievement-oriented players. Rod Laver feels his concentration sharpen when he's behind. Laver is no less achievement-oriented for being a late starter. He needs to win; needs to win all of the time. "After all," he says, "once you're behind, it's either play better or lose, isn't it?" Margaret Court is another player whose speed, strength, and coordination can suddenly mesh gears when she is behind; and then there's no stopping her. Evonne Goolagong Cawley—who is famous for her lapses of concentration—often falls behind, but a couple of winners can spur her on. Her great natural ability then can carry her to win several games running.

Another simple but effective rule which many pros follow is: "Never let yourself believe you're winning until it's all over." In the 1974 final at Wimbledon, for example, Jimmy Connors played an aggressive, almost savage match against Ken Rosewall, never letting up on him even at the last point. Connors was asked, hadn't he any pity for "poor Ken"? "I've seen people pity Ken Rosewall and lose," he answered, in an obvious reference to the semifinal match that Rosewall had won against Stan Smith the day before. Smith had taken two sets and had the third pretty much in his pocket when Rosewall caught fire.

Concentration

A club or college player may do poorly for a while—perhaps a couple of double faults, or netting some overheads—but then, when well behind, he will suddenly become looser and hit the ball deeper and faster. He often goes on to win the set or match. What is involved is the sudden sharpening of negative motivation. The psyche says, "We're losing anyway, so why play it safe? Let's go down in a blaze of glory, with a few winners at least." And so the player loosens his swing and hits harder. He is often amazed when he finds that he has won several games.

Conversely, this same club or college team player may start off by winning the first three games, allow the intensity of his concentration to diminish, and then proceed to lose the next four games. Here we are dealing with a distinct lapse in concentration brought on by diminished motivation, which, in turn, is brought on by overconfidence.

The Japanese masters of the martial arts rightly contend that anxiety is the major foe of concentration. Such masters utilize both staying loose and focusing beyond as ways to diminish distraction. They do this by (1) keeping relaxed those muscles which are not critical to the focus of concentration, and (2) changing from narrow focus to broad focus to relaxation, as called for. A few Western athletes have instinctively learned this technique. Joe Louis had a deadpan face, with every muscle of expression relaxed. Great backs like Jim Brown and O. J. Simpson get up slowly after a tackle. Ann Haydon Jones allows her racket and both her arms to hang until just before the ball is hit toward her.

Intense concentration need not be inimical to a free swing. The top tennis pros concentrate with their *eyes*. They allow the body in motion to perform as perfectly as it has so many times in practice. Evonne Goolagong Cawley and Bjorn Borg perfectly illustrate this coordination of physical motion and visual concentration.

Bjorn Borg demonstrates intense physical and mental coordination, yet shows no sign of anxiety, as he concentrates on the ball.

Evonne Goolagong combines freedom of body movement with intensity of concentration.

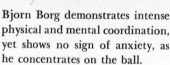

We lesser lights of the tennis firmament can also use concentration to enhance a strong, free arm motion. First our arms and bodies must know the proper moves. Then our eyes can watch the ball intently, allowing no sensory or mental distraction. The swing will be smooth and consistent, and if we cannot all be Borgs and Goolagongs we will at least have risen a little toward those stars.

CHAPTER FOUR

Fitness

IN tennis, there is more to fitness than the wind and muscle training which produces strength and endurance. Tennis fitness is a combination of training and skill: the achieved ability to move and hit fast and accurate shots in minimal time with minimal motion.

Here, the psychological factors—motivation, anxiety, and concentration—play both a supporting and a deciding role. Each dictates how well the physically readied muscles, heart, and lungs will perform. Physical training does the rest.

The Skill Factor

Efficiency of technique—the skill factor—is of critical importance to the tennis player. With efficient technique, the player can perform at a lower heart and respiratory rate because his working muscles are expending a lesser amount of energy per work load, and his nonworking muscles are as close to rest as possible. Since skill is a psychophysiological factor, it is more difficult to measure than are physiological functions; the treadmill and the bicycle ergometer will not show it. But skill is a common denominator in the mastery of all sports.

The novice-to-intermediate player will find, when up against a tough opponent, that he feels "tight." His body will look tight; his motions will be jerky rather than fluid, and he will use too many of them too much of the time. In contrast, the expert will use only those muscles needed for the actual playing motions. The other muscles of his body will be relaxed. He will look "loose."

Although the motivation of the less experienced, less efficient player may be equal to that of the expert, his anxiety level will be higher, and this anxiety will play upon his inefficiently trained body. He will be both physically and emotionally tense. Both his mind and his body will be working against his winning.

One part of the attainment of efficiency of technique is motivated, concentrated, low-anxiety practice; the other part is motivated, concentrated, low-anxiety development of strength and endurance. The player's tools for the development of these primarily physiological factors are his muscles, heart, and lungs.

Muscles

All muscle tissue has the characteristics of contractibility and response to electrical stimuli and chemical mediators. Beyond these basics, the three types of muscle tissue—striated, smooth, and cardiac—are purpose-specific.

Striated muscle moves the body. Capable of rapid contraction with great force, it is the body's performance medium. With few exceptions, striated muscle is voluntary muscle, moving at conscious command. The muscles of the trunk, limbs, head, and neck—all are voluntary.

Striated (or skeletal) muscle does more than swing the racket. As it does so, it sets in motion an immense complex of supportive activity: rate and volume increases in respiration, increases in heart rate and in the return of venous blood to the heart, dilation of the blood vessels of the muscles, and constriction of the blood vessels of the skin and digestive system. On this muscle tissue and support system the player's strength and much of his endurance, speed, and reaction time depend.

Smooth muscle is involuntary muscle. It will not respond to conscious command and does not respond to conventional training. Because it will not and does not do these things, this muscle tissue is often given short shrift by the athlete. But smooth muscle is important to athletic performance. Found in the organs of the digestive tract and in the bronchioles, it is, more pertinently, also found in the blood vessels. Thus, smooth muscle controls the flow of blood to the athlete's striated muscle. When the tennis player finds, at the end of the fifth set (the third or fourth, for some of us) that his muscle fatigue is so great that his arm can swing the racket only fast enough to meet the ball in back of the midbody line, this is because the metabolic oxygen requirements of striated, voluntary muscle are not being met by the blood supply carried by smooth, involuntary muscle tissue.

Cardiac muscle has two characteristics directly relevant to a player's speed, strength, and endurance. First, unlike skeletal muscle, cardiac muscle cannot get along for any appreciable period without oxygen. Second, while ventilation can increase twenty-five times and the oxygen consumption of skeletal muscle tissue can increase from fifteen to twenty times over resting values, the cardiovascular machinery in the middle of the oxygen transport system cannot increase output by even ten times resting values. Heart rate can increase only three times, and stroke volume twice. Therefore, much of the player's strength and endurance depends upon the efficiency with which his pulmonary, cardiovascular, and muscle systems can be made to operate within the confines of these heart-set limitations.

Sudden bursts of concentrated activity, such as those immediately involved in the startle reaction or in a sprinter's first moves, require no preliminary work on the part of the lungs, heart, and circulatory system. Evolutionary development has resulted in a body prepared for either fight or flight. The body keeps itself constantly ready for immediate, violently powerful, short bursts of work (1) by keeping a small reserve supply of oxygen, held in the blood by hemoglobin and in the muscles by myoglobin, and (2) by requiring no oxygen for the first stage of muscle energy metabolism to take place. Remarkably, a sprinter can do 100 yards without any oxygen at all; and although it is doubtful that a runner's muscles could last half a mile without oxygen, he probably could hold his breath for two minutes at rest.

In addition to energy, this airless first-stage process, called anaerobic metabolism, produces lactic acid, the substance directly responsible for much of the pain and stiffness which can develop in the poorly trained and overused striated muscle. In order for the muscle to continue to function effectively, it is necessary for its lactic acid content to be broken down and done away with.

Oxygen becomes necessary when a portion of the anaerobically produced lactic acid is transformed into carbon dioxide, water, and additional energy. At this point begins aerobic (or oxygen-utilizing) metabolism—a process fifteen to twenty times more efficient in energy formation than its anaerobic progenitor.

Pulmonary and Cardiovascular Systems

The lungs, heart, and circulatory system are long-haul mechanisms. Cardiac muscle cannot contract with the explosiveness of striated (or skeletal) muscle, but the strongest skeletal muscle cannot match the endurance of the heart for even a few days, let alone a lifetime.

In any specific situation, the rapidity and much of the efficiency with which these portions of the body's oxygen transport system function depends upon the balance between the amount of oxygen and the amount of carbon dioxide in the blood. Under normal circumstances, this balance is governed to a large extent by the amount of work being done by the striated muscles.

By means of an increase in rate and volume of respiration, and an increase in heart rate and per stroke volume, the heart and lungs supply the increased need of the working muscles for oxygen. The alternating contractions of the working muscles act as a pump to send blood back to the heart.

Getting It Together

When you walk out on the court, toss up that first ball, and hit it, that tossing and hitting necessitate a series of contractions of striated muscle tissue. Although the muscle tissue involved normally contains some reserve oxygen, the amount is really not much more than will allow you to walk onto the court swinging your racket, take your position, toss up that first ball, and hit it. If you are going to continue playing, you must get some oxygen into those working muscles very soon.

Otherwise, not only will you be unable to hit that ball which is coming toward you across the net, but you will not even be able to move to meet it.

With the first contractions involved in tossing and hitting, the blood vessels in each of the affected skeletal muscles expand. The degree to which they expand depends directly upon the strength of their muscle's contraction—how fast and how hard you have hit. The degree to which these blood vessels expand determines the amount of oxygen that can be carried into the muscles and the amount of carbon dioxide that can be carried off. In turn, the strength and number of muscle contractions—how hard, how fast, and how long you play—dictate how much muscle energy will be needed. That need determines how much oxygen must get in—so that what started out as a piece of whole wheat bread can be converted into the quick run and the smash of racket against ball —and, as a result of that conversion, how much carbon dioxide must be disposed of.

As the game continues, an imbalance soon develops between the amounts of oxygen and carbon dioxide in the blood. The inevitably increased proportion of carbon dioxide triggers two sets of mechanisms signaling the lungs to breathe faster and deeper, and the heart to pump faster and harder, so as to increase the amount of oxygen and restore this vital balance.

The first set of mechanisms, with its signals activated in the contracting muscles and relayed via the nervous system, has an "act now" effect. The second set is slower, activated by a threatened alteration in brain chemistry, and has primarily a "get ready for later" effect. You will become conscious of its workings at the end of the game when, for a time after you have stopped playing and are at rest, you are still breathing hard and your heart is still pounding.

When the store of muscle glycogen edges toward depletion

and the rate of increase in the carbon dioxide level gets to the point where, because of the limitations of the heart, it cannot be dealt with effectively, the player becomes tired, slows down, and (if wise) will stop playing.

So far as the muscles and their oxygen transport system is concerned, that would seem to be all there is to the game. But even here, something more is happening. During the course of playing, practice, and exercise, changes occur in the lungs, heart, and muscle tissue which can lead to that much sought after, taut but fluid, always at-the-ready condition which we call physical fitness.

Physical Fitness

The physically fit individual can handle a larger work load for a longer time at lower heart and respiratory rates than the untrained, nonfit individual can. What enables him to perform better? The answer is an increase in his oxygen utilization capacity. In effect, fitness is a combination of improvements in the efficiency of the lungs, heart, and striated muscle. Each involves an increase in volume of blood flow.

The increase in respiratory function results in an amplification of the positive and, especially, the negative pressures within the chest. These pressures assist the blood flow to the heart through the great veins of the chest. The working striated muscles also enhance blood return. The heart becomes more efficient in delivering the greater amount of blood it receives. Each contraction pumps a greater volume of blood.

Although the mild to moderate exercise of tennis does not increase stroke volume, it does increase heart rate. This increase helps the heart deliver more blood and improves the tone and contractile states of the heart muscle. Thus, each contraction of the ventricles sends the blood out faster, allowing greater time for refilling.

The more numerous intracellular sites of oxygen utilization (mitochondria) which come with physical conditioning enable the muscles in which they develop to extract more oxygen from the blood. The result is that the blood returned to the heart and sent to the lungs contains comparatively less oxygen. Together with improved respiratory function, this accounts for a larger arterial-venous oxygen difference—a routinely measurable sign of physical fitness.

Increased Strength and Endurance

Improvements in strength and endurance come with proper use of striated and cardiac muscle. The striated muscles of greatest importance for tennis are those which move the hand and arm. Strength in these muscles is developed through use, and is necessary not only for power but also for control.

More helpful than playing hours and hours of tennis is making these muscles work against increasing loads. Since their enlargement will be in proportion to the strength of contraction, rather than its duration, maximal load training is most productive. Hand springs, old tennis balls, weights, or any other method using the overload principle, in which muscles are exercised against near maximum resistance, will strengthen them faster and further than tennis playing alone will.

Isometric strength building is a marked departure from all previous conceptions of exercise. Its name comes from the fact that, during contraction, the muscle length is not changed. Isometric muscle strengthening exercises use maximal resistance without bodily movement. The muscles work against an immovable object, such as a wall or doorway, or against muscles pushing in the opposite direction. Isometric exercises increase muscle strength markedly and quickly, but they do not contribute to cardiovascular conditioning. In fact, sharp elevations of blood pressure can accompany isometrics.

Fitness

Fitness per se can elevate one's game moderately. Tennis, after all, is not marathon running. Fitness, however, applies not only to muscle, lungs, and blood but also to the psyche. The fit individual has a better self-image. He exhibits greater self-confidence and less anxiety.

Fitness plus the secondary psychological factors can boost one's game a full level or more.

CHAPTER FIVE

Precision

PRECISION has several components: how objects and movements seem to appear and seem to feel, the degree to which they are remembered, and the way they are remembered as appearing and feeling. Learning is involved. So is decision-making, the calling up of perceived and remembered material so as to select what elements will be used in any particular act.

Perception

The physical characteristics of objects and events become known to us by means of sensory perception. In tennis, visual perception is the most frequently used means of obtaining this information.

The organization of visual perception is complex; at any given moment, what one "sees" is prey to a myriad of distorting factors. Physical factors, such as the size, shape, and color of the focal object, the presence or absence of adjacent objects, and the characteristics of the background, influence one's visual perception. Internal psychophysiological states, such as degree of motivation, level of awareness, and degree of concentration, as well as the physiological characteristics of binocular vision, also exert varying degrees of influence.

The elements of visual perception include perspective, distance, and several primarily psychological phenomena. Most of both the type and degree of perceptual accuracy involved in tennis is learned by the player through practice and actual play.

Perspective

Perspective depends on a number of factors, such as light, distance, and angle of vision. Objects in the foreground are perceived as being larger, sharper, more vivid in color; they usually block out more distant objects in the same line of vision. Lines converge toward a vanishing point in the distance, and circles become ovals as the angle of view departs from the perpendicular. Objects in close proximity to one another will seem to merge, as one's distance from them increases.

The thing to remember is that when some of these "known" characteristics of perspective are not in accord with others, illusions can occur. Since the Renaissance, artists have represented reality through the created illusion of reality, rather than through a precise copying of nature. They have consciously employed a learned repertoire of line and color distortions whose purpose is to trick the viewer into "seeing" what he has learned to perceive as reality.

Distance

The size of an object perceived at a distance is related not so much to its actual distance from us as to what we have learned to perceive that distance to be. The thing to remember here is that if what one perceives varies from known experience, illusions occur.

An anthropological study of a tribe of African forest pygmies illustrates the point. Since the dense tropical forest in which the tribe lives provides little opportunity for seeing any distance greater than a few yards, few judgments are based on the members' perception of distance. Thus, when one pygmy accompanied an anthropologist to an open plain where, in the distance, many buffalo were grazing, the forest pygmy "saw" the buffalo as beetles, and nothing could convince him otherwise. Similarly, it is not unusual for a child on his or her first plane trip to look down on a city or town and believe the houses and cars a few thousand feet below to be toys.

Distance perception is to a large extent a function of binocular vision, which, in turn, is the result of three mechanisms: convergence, convexity, and interpretation. In convergence, as an object approaches, the extraocular muscles positioning the eyeballs "feel" the distance by contraction. Convexity means that as each eye focuses on the approaching object, its lens becomes more convex. The convexity of the lens is under the control of the ciliary muscle, which also "feels" the distance at which the lens focuses. Finally, since each eye sees the object from a slightly different angle, the two images differ slightly. They are integrated in the brain and "interpreted" for distance.

Because of the differences in the physical angles involved, we tend to make poor estimates of the size and speed of objects at distances of more than twenty-five or thirty feet, but rather accurate ones of those within five or six feet. This is more a matter of physics than of physiology. For example, to focus a 35mm camera from twenty feet to infinity requires only a small movement of the lens, while focusing from ten feet to three feet requires a considerable extension of the lens. The eyes, too, make only small adjustments to focus from twenty feet to infinity, but require greater adjustments from ten feet to three feet. The eye muscles "feel" the larger changes more easily and more accurately. Similar ratios exist for distance versus closeness, relative to the convergence angles of the two eyes and the image differences between the right and left eye.

Perception can also be influenced by distraction, acclimatization and accentuation, all of which play important roles in tennis and all of which are, for the most part, psychological phenomena.

Distraction

Recognizing from their own experience that concentration can be maintained only by shutting out extraneous stimuli, the more flamboyant players among the pros often employ a repertoire of antics aimed at shifting their opponent's focus by means of the unexpected.

Some players employ a somewhat exaggerated motion in their serve and other strokes. The excess motion will tend to cause the receiving player to judge the initial velocity to be faster than it actually is. Other players employ a smooth, apparently effortless motion which tends to cause the receiving player to underestimate the initial velocity.

The two opponents in the finals of the 1975 Fireman's Fund International Tournament, Guillermo Vilas and Arthur Ashe, present an interesting contrast in this respect. Vilas is strong and well muscled. His serves use the force of his body as part of their power source. Since Ashe has a slim body, he uses the whip of his arm to develop speed in his serve. His serve is actually faster than Vilas', and its speed is deceptive. This factor, as much as velocity, accounts for many of Ashe's frequent aces.

Acclimatization

Unchanging stimuli diminish in effectiveness and tend to become part of the background. The recipient of such constant stimuli, his level of awareness consequently lowered, becomes lulled into behaving as though they will always be there. Such stimuli can be quite gross. For example, people living near airports cease to be aware of the sound of planes on regular flight patterns.

The removal of a stimulus to which one has become acclimatized can be effectively distracting, as the following incident proves. It was the habit of Charles F. Pope, the organist for a neighborhood church, to play improvisations and background music as the congregation arrived. The congregation was a talkative one, and the conversations of its members generally overshadowed the music. One Sunday, as he played, Charles gradually raised the volume of the music. The conversations grew louder. The music grew louder. The conversations grew even louder. When both were at many decibels, Charles abruptly stopped the music, thereby allowing the people to hear themselves shouting at each other.

Then there was silence.

There are instances when repetition evokes not acclimatization but impatience and anxiety. Harold Solomon, tennis' human backboard, will return groundstroke after groundstroke until his opponent becomes exasperated enough to try to put one away. His opponents usually make more errors than they hit winners.

Both distraction and acclimatization are dependent upon the ego needs as well as the psychophysiological idiosyncrasies of the individual. We know a poet, a sometime lyricist for a rock band, who cannot write poetry if baroque or other classical music is playing in the background. Because this is his favorite type of music, he can be distracted by it. It fights for his attention with the rhythms of his words and lines. Conversely, this poet has written some successful rock lyrics while in a small studio with the band rehearsing at full volume. In contrast to classical music, he hears rock as mere background noise.

Accentuation

Accentuation is the tendency for the characteristics of a desired object to become more vivid to the perceiver. Purely subjective, fired by motivation, this distortion is the direct result of heightened awareness. Research examples of this phenomenon range from poor Boston children who consistently overestimate the size of coins to winner players who, with their concentration sharply focused, actually see the ball as more sharply delineated, more intense in color, than it normally appears to be.

The thing to remember is that perception is selective. From moment to moment, need filters the vast array of sights, sounds, and moves which the brain takes in. In term of visual perception, so important in tennis, the momentary hierarchy of psychophysiological needs dictates not only what is seen but how it is seen. This hierarchy is dictated, in turn, by motivation and concentration. Motivation dictates what will be seen and why it will be seen. Concentration dictates how much of it will be seen and what it will seem to look like.

Memory

Fed by perception and modified by language and subsequent experience, memory is directly associated with learning and, hence, with the problem-solving and decision-making involved in the situational creativity of tennis.

Forms of Remembered Material

Material is generally stored in and recalled from memory in one of two basic forms, words or sensations.

The fancy way of saying that words are stored in memory

is to say that what is in or up there is symbolic memory, verbally encoded. No matter what it is called, verbal memory is still a multitude of sets of words. Those pertinent to winning tennis are for the most part sets of directions as to the execution of specific moves. Sensory data, including all the visual imagery so important to tennis and so directly involved in perception, are also stored in memory.

Perhaps even more important to tennis are the kinesthetic data stored there. These include the "feel" of the move and the "moves" of the moves—the entire complex of sensations associated with the simultaneous and serial workings of bones, muscles, tendons, and ligaments in motion, as they execute a specific act in a series of specific acts, such as walking out onto the court, tossing a tennis ball up into the air, and hitting it.

Retention of much kinesthetic data is extremely long-lasting. Individuals who once knew how to hit an overhead smash, or do a tip roll on skis or a wheelie on a motor bike, or any of hundreds of other complex body maneuvers, will tend to retain some recall of the moves. Either they will remember how to perform the motion by means of kinesthetic recall, or they will be able to relearn it rapidly and easily.

Types of Memory

The senses transmit an overwhelming number of items of information to the brain. Under proper conditions, stimuli of less than a millisecond in duration can be perceived and remembered. There are three distinct types of memory. In increasing order of duration, they are sensory residual memory, short-term memory, and long-term memory.

Sensory residual memory is, as the name implies, an afterimage. Sensory residual memory is evanescent. Its consciously perceived existence is very brief—less than half a second. For example, the player who sees the impact of ball on racket will continue to "see" the ball on the strings for an additional fraction of a second. But, in general, he will never again be consciously aware of that image, will never be able to bring to recall the actual sensory occurrence of that event of less than a half second's duration. Of course, although the individual image may be extinguished, a seccession of such images can have a longer lasting, cumulative effect.

Short-term memory is interpretive—the "knowing" of what has been perceived. Short-term memory holds information for time spans ranging from a few seconds to few minutes. Most of this information is then "lost." Like the contents of sensory residual memory, short-term memory items become irretrievable to conscious awareness. However, some of the data are transferred to long-term memory, from which, even years later, they can be retrieved.

Improving Your Memory

The tennis player's most compelling interest in memory, per se, concerns methods by which items held in short-term memory can be implanted in long-term memory, as well as techniques through which long-term memory can be reinforced to the point where recall is fast and foolproof.

Items from short-term memory are most efficiently implanted in long-term memory in accordance with this rule: Keep it *small*. Keep it *short*. Keep it *significant*. And, through it all, concentrate.

The nature of what is to be remembered influences the chances of its entry into long-term memory. The more personally significant the information is, the more likely is its chance of being remembered. Therefore, the more important tennis is to the player, the greater the likelihood of his remembering the specific moves involved.

Since both conditions enhance concentration, being motivated and being aroused also exert an influence on memory. The conditions under which information enters short-term memory can determine whether and how well that information will be fixed in long-term memory. For example, if the gathering of information to be recalled is immediately followed by some other concentrated intellectual activity, competitive inhibition occurs and retention will be minimal. But if information gathering is followed by sleep or minimal cerebral cortical activity, memory will not be inhibited.

Thus, the drilling on one stroke should not be followed immediately by drilling on another. Each segment of learning should be followed by rest and quiet. When the strokes are well learned and it is time to use them in sequence, the combinations should be simple. Only later, when the strokes and simple sequences are so firmly implanted that they are down pat, should unique and intricate types of combinations be attempted.

Items stored in long-term memory stand a better chance of remaining useful if they are reinforced by means of relation, reduction, repetition, and rehearsal. Information is more likely to be retained in a usable form if it is woven into an existing framework of knowledge—that is, if it is related to what is already known or more firmly implanted. If the material is reduced to its essence, and the key words, phrases, and sets of movements are concentrated upon, the reinforced essence will tend to carry its "surround" with it into recall. Repetition by means of speaking or writing, by concentrating on a mental image, and by teaching the material to others are all effective methods of reinforcement. Finally, the more rehearsal or re-enactment of the event or set of motions, the greater its chance of retention, and the greater the amount of accurately recalled detail which will accompany it.

There are two types of recall from long-term memory. The first is rote—the item is recalled directly as an entity. The second is reconstruction—the item is remembered within the context of related events. Both types are used repeatedly and instantaneously in every tennis game. Rote memory's prime function is in the execution of each specific move. Reconstructed memory functions in analytic thought—in recalling which move learned by rote was best used in which series of moves in a similar situation in a previous match.

How Memory Happens

The cerebral cortex is the substrate of thought, learning, and creativity. Each of the roughly 12 billion neurons it contains connects with dozens of its comrades to form an integrated network of electrical pathways throughout the six major layers of the cortex. Ideas, memory, backhand technique, strategy—all thought processes are the result of electrical impulses traveling particular nerve pathways in the cortex.

An impulse representing such mental activity does not travel over a chain of single nerve cell fibers connected in a series. Rather, there is a wavelike advance of impulses over several nerve fibers and across several synapses, in parallel. The more rooted the thought or body of knowledge, the wider the wave.

In order to picture what happens—and, for the sake of simplification, neglecting such factors as inhibitory influences and input from other brain centers—think of the waves of electrical activity which stand for the mental activity involved in thought, learning, and creativity as a procession of automobiles traveling side by side down a multilane highway. The highway does not run as the crow flies but, rather, along the equivalent of scenic routes. Sometimes, one or two cars in the group find their way onto a dead-end street off the main highway. At other times, the highway divides; further on, it becomes one again. At one or more points, a few lanes may leave the highway to circle around; still further on, they rejoin it.

These circulatory excursions are called reverberatory circuits. They are functionally important because parts of the impulse wave presumably travel around the reverberatory circuit a number of times before traversing the rest of the pathway. Thus, the excitation of that pathway system is maintained for a greater length of time.

When an image is remembered, the electrical impulse must travel the same basic pathway as it did the time before. With each use of a given pathway, a change occurs which makes it easier for subsequent impulse waves to use it. The reverberatory circuits help to provide an extra measure of use.

In tennis, the more times a player has hit a perfect backhand, the more firmly the coordination and timing are remembered by the brain circuits, and the more easily the same nerve pathways will produce a perfect backhand the next time.

As the same memory is repeatedly called up, facilitative changes occur at the synaptic junctions between the neurons in the pathway. The end result is a path of least resistance called an engram. It has been theorized that a creative mind possesses an unusually great complexity of engrams which have been set down by a generous variety of experience and thought, and that, in addition, such a brain weaves inventive engram designs with unusual ease. A creative "tennis brain" must first have the circuits involved in the shots, tactics, and changes of playing style indelibly embedded, so as to draw upon them creatively.

Learning

Skillful tennis is primarily the product of sensorimotor learning, and repetition plays a major role in its acquisition. Sensorimotor learning is the first type of learning to develop in the infant, and is its total world until around the age of two.

Precision

Sensorimotor learning is an ongoing process, often reaching, in adults, a high state of sophistication in such diverse activities as wine-tasting, surgery, and athletics.

Although the child goes on to develop internalized thought and learning, eventually learns to think with symbols as well as sensations, and may even learn the intricacies of logic and conceptual thought, he never loses his need to master sensorimotor skills, which are also the basis of learning in tennis.

Types of Learning

Human learning occurs primarily by means of repetition, association, trial and error, and analytic thought, e.g., the application of rules and principles. The first, repetition, is merely rote learning. It goes into memory as such and comes out as rote memory. You do what you are told to do, you remember you were told or what you did, and then you do it again. Rote learning is as simple as that.

In tennis, learning by association takes three major forms: dependence, contingency, and magic.

· Dependence: If the racket head is forward of the hand when the ball is struck, the shot will be ipso facto across the court. The second event is a necessary consequence of the first.

· Contingency: Hit a flat serve flat out and the probability of its going in will be considerably less than 100 percent. The second event is a likely but not a necessary consequence of the first.

· Magic: A match is won easily while the player is wearing a certain piece of clothing, or after he or she has performed a certain ritual. Although there is no necessary or probable connection between the two events, the player, combining coincidence and superstition, assumes a "magical" cause-and-effect relationship.

Many serious players, though they be bright, sensible,

charming, and witty, harbor some small, irrational belief. Possessed of an intense need to excel, yet at the same time knowing that they are fallible, they resort to calling upon what Freud termed "the magic helper"—some specific childhood object or essence brought into adulthood to facilitate the attainment of the desired goal.

Eli Wallach, for example, never tucks his shirt into his tennis shorts. A player we know will not complete a 360° turn on the court. If she does so, she must unwind herself by completely turning around the other way. Another player we know has two Head rackets, identical except for the color of the handle. Blindfolded she cannot tell them apart, but she invariably plays better with the brown-handled one.

Gardnar Mulloy never uncovers his racket before he walks onto the court for a match. Frew McMillan never plays without his cap. Frew says that the cap is his "security blanket." Roy Emerson is said to have worn the same pair of shorts in every tournament match for a year. It was one of his best years. More generally, many pros will avoid stepping on any of the lines of the court before, after, or between games.

One of the more bizarre cases of magical learning arose when Olga Morozova borrowed a red wristband during the final rounds of the 1974 Virginia Slims tournament. She beat Rosemary Casals in the semifinals and faced Billie Jean King in the finals. Olga neglected to wear the red wristband early in the match, after she took a 3–0 lead on two service breaks. Billie Jean won the next two games. Olga then put on the red wristband. Olga won the match. Or did the red wristband win it? Or was the real winner the magic creature from whom Olga had borrowed the magic red wristband?

The third major type of learning, *trial and error,* is exactly what the name implies. First attempts at learning new skills usually employ this method. The individual brings modes of behavior learned by rote out of memory and applies them to a new situation. After learning basic form, the beginning tennis player must use trial and error to fine-tune perception, in order to accurately judge the speed of the oncoming ball.

Analytic thought, the fourth and last type, involves the trial-and-error application of information previously learned by rote, association, and trial and error, and assembled by means of simple, step-by-step logic.

The fundamentals are these: When confronted by a situation in which previously learned, memory-stored, routinely brought out and used patterns of thought and behavior do not work, the individual mentally "backs off" from the situation and mentally inspects its contents. Then, usually within the context of the basic rules and principles that he has learned to apply to the situation or to one like it, he summons up as much relevant information as possible, mentally lists alternative solutions, weighs the chances of each one, and then tries out the alternative with the best chance of success.

This is a five-step process which the cortex is capable of executing almost instantaneously: (1) inspect, (2) list, (3) weigh, (4) decide and (5) try. If successful, proceed. If unsuccessful, go back. Then, reinspect, relist (discarding the redundant alternative), reassess, decide, and try again. And so on . . . until either success comes or frustration at lack of success causes abandonment of the procedure. The successful alternative is stored in memory, from whence it may be summoned and reapplied to the same or a related problem in subsequent experience.

In tennis, most analytic thought is never translated into words. Instead, it consists of muscle movements and kinesthetic sensations. Except when used in mapping out strategy or a series of moves, as in chess, football, or short sequences of tennis, most analytic word thought does not occur on an acutely conscious level.

Rudimentary use of analytic thought begins quite early. Its fundamentals are usually learned through imitation of authority figures, i.e., parents, older siblings, and teachers. Some of the first times an individual applies the analytic method to motor activity are when he or she learns how to eat with a spoon, button buttons, and tie shoelaces. A crucial moment in the use of analytic thought to psychically manipulate the outside world comes when, after grabs, tears, and screams, the child hits on the alternative of smiling while saying "Please."

With age, experience, and practice, the use of analytic thought becomes more frequent and the solutions—at least, to minor problems—come faster. Analytic thought and its execution as motor activity constitute the best method for learning groups of continuous motor skills. In tennis, the learning method is generally called practice.

The difficulties encountered by the individual engaging in analytic thought are generally flaws of assessment: problems in assigning relative weights, or degrees of importance, to the alternatives in step 3. Magic and outmoded patterns of thought and behavior usually tend to be given undue weight as alternatives, and produce inefficient decision-making in step 4.

The tennis player may not be aware of all his errors in grip, foot position, arm extension, racket position at impact, or any of the many other kinesthetic requisites to consistent, winning tennis. He thus may not be able to carry out the rest of the analytic thought process in correcting his form and game. A coach—even if the relationship is informal—can point out such errors, and then the player can proceed analytically to correct his strokes.

It is not shameful to need a coach's eye. Few of us see ourselves accurately, whether it be on a tennis court or in a social milieu. The touring professionals themselves receive coaching on a continual basis. Remember: correct observation of how we play must precede evaluation. Evaluation must precede decision-making.

Optimization

Some sports involve little decision-making. In others, the decisions never stop. Where competition is primarily against an absolute—time, distance, or the performance of some feat —decision-making is not a major factor. But in sports involving direct interaction between competitors, decisions are continual. Of these sports, tennis is one of the most demanding.

Every shot involves so many variables that the number of combinations is virtually endless. The speed of the ball is one factor. Then there are the many factors related to how the ball can be hit. Topspin? Underspin? Flat? The shot can be deep or short, to a corner or down the middle, a lob or drive or overhead. Where is the sun? What about the wind? Of course, all these variables are not independent (not even Roscoe Tanner can hit a 140-mile-an-hour lob!), but there are still more factors influencing the tennis player's decision. These include the position of the opponent, the levels of ability of player and opponent, the specific strengths and weaknesses of each, and the whims of each. There are intuition, superstition, and "grandmothers' tales" to be taken into account.

And, with the exception of the serve, the total time for each decision is about a second.

The aim of the individual with a decision to make is to pick the alternative with the greatest chance of success. This is called optimization.

Logic would lead one to predict that at any given moment, any given individual will select the alternative which is most likely to accord him or her the greatest benefit. But life is seldom so logical, and human decision-making is never that straightforward. What is optimal for one person may not be so for another; and what is optimal for the same person at one time may not be so at another.

The "greatest benefit" is not an absolute. It is only greatest relative to the values attributed to other alternatives. The value attributed to each alternative is subjective and dependent upon a host of variables. Disparate, often seemingly irrelevant, these variables range from the psychological idiosyncrasies of the individual, whether he won at tennis the last time he played (or the last time he played against his present opponent), and whether he is tired or depressed, to his family history, his economic status, and the present contents of his stomach.

Probability

Once values have been assigned to various choices, the decision is based on probabilities, or estimations of likelihood. These, too, are not absolute. They can be influenced by such intervening personal variables as optimism, pessimism, and pragmatism.

Probability not only influences decision but decisions also influence probabilities. For example, if you expect an individual whom you are about to meet to be a warm person, yóur reaction upon meeting him is likely to evoke warmth. This is a self-fulfilling prophecy.

Only once removed from the self-fulfilling prophecy is decision-making based on the knowledge and thinking of one's adversary. The probability is that if you base your decision on such "knowledge," you also will probably decide that your adversary's decision will, in turn, be based on his estimation of your judgment of his knowledge. You soon find yourself in the circular trap of "He knows that I know that he knows that. . . ." Where do you stop? If you pursue this line of thought too far, you might just as well toss a coin.

What you decide that your opponent knows can only be based on your highly subjective analysis, and is therefore most probably not only exaggerated but also fallacious. It is therefore rather likely that if you choose this route, you are beaten before you start. It is probably best to concentrate on what you know and leave the guesswork to your opponent.

An additional complication is that you are dealing not only with relative values but also with risks. Often the choice holding the promise of the greatest reward is the one accompanied by the gravest risk.

What to Do?

Suppose your opponent has come to the net behind a shot to your forehand corner. You can try to pass him down the line, pass him cross court, lob, or hit right at him.

· There are probability ranges for each of your shot's chances of going in.
· There are probabilities for your opponent's chances of putting away your return.
· There are probabilities for your return's being a winner.
· The drive at the opponent is most likely to be in, but also most likely to be hit back as a winner.
· The passing shot is least likely to go in; but if it does, it is most likely to be a winner.

Add to these difficulties the one-second time limit for making the decision, and what are you, the poor tennis player, to do? No, you cannot sit down on the baseline and suck your thumb.

Increased objectivity at the outset (step 1 : inspect) is part of the solution.

In tennis, a combination of preparation, motivation, concentration, a hot racket, and a cool head will tend to help you, because the answer lies in your having gained the experience of playing enough tennis to have been in this situation many times before. Court sense (or presence, or situational creativity) is the result of learning in the form of much drill, much objective analysis, and hard years on the courts. With drill, analysis, and practice, optimization becomes as close to automatic as any choice can get, and probabilities will lose much of their equivocality.

Tennis Zen

Attempts at applying the Zen method of learning to tennis have received much recent attention. The Zen method abandons the traditional way of learning by parts, and substitutes the steps of (1) observation, (2) visualization, and (3) allowing the body to perform the strokes. Conscious thought is not involved. It is contended that conscious thought inhibits proper stroke production.

This method of learning by wholes has been used for some time, in an informal way, by many individuals in many sports. Its most universal application is taken for granted: teenagers learning the latest dance step.

Zen is no shortcut. In the United States, form and perfection are secondary to results and the speed with which they can be achieved. In contrast, the Zen learning concept is Eastern in origin, advocated by Oriental masters who have never tried to hurry their learning of any physical activity. Nor are they interested in results; form and perfection are their goals.

A parable illustrates the Zen attitude. A beginning archer does not string the arrow on the bow until he learns to take the arrow out of the quiver. Learning the proper form of quiver extraction may take weeks, hundreds of trials, and infinite patience. When the novice advances to the stage of releasing the arrow from the taut bow, it does not matter—as long as the form is perfect—whether he actually hits the target. When form is truly perfect, the arrow will seem to have willed itself to the bullseye.

Learning by wholes is no panacea for the poor novice. It will not miraculously transform his strokes into laser-like missiles. The Zen method requires the player to work on form until he can "feel" the correct swing. Once he is at the point, he can form a sensory image, as much proprioceptive as visual, and then allow his body to follow that image. In order for the body to carry out the image without distraction, the holistic theorists suggest concentrating on some object, such as the ball.

Watch the ball? While tennis has always relied on mysticism, the Zen tennis people have added a refinement by claiming that since the spherical form of the ball is patently uninteresting, what one must watch is the ball's seams and the ball's arc of flight. In concentrating on the ball, it is best not to translate that effort into verbal terms, such as "Watch the ball, dummy." Rather, the effort must be visual and thus direct.

Simplified, the steps of the holistic method are: (1) repeated observation, (2) patient work on form, (3) forming a sensory image, and (4) allowing the body to perform.

The holistic method can be effective. It is not necessary to be a purist, however. Small correction of *parts* of the stroke can be used in step 2, and the player can return to steps 1 and 2 for corrective work even after he is somewhat proficient at steps 3 and 4.

As with all other influences on his game, the player must evaluate what he brings to the game and which methods, or method mix, will bring out his best.

A portion of Occidental tennis advice parallels Eastern lines of thought: the serious player is taught to analyze his play and that of others in terms of percentages, typical errors, and other strategic considerations. Above all, he must observe—not merely watch. He must also think about tennis while away from the courts, as when daydreaming at work. Once this information is programmed in the brain, it can then be used for the split-second decisions of the match. Just as in Eastern thought, the mind and body are thus taught to function "automatically."

CHAPTER SIX

Situational Creativity

ALL truly great tennis players are capable of situational creativity. This is not the creativity of a Michelangelo or a Bach; rather, it is a more everyday, reactively creative process.

In tennis, situational creativity evidences itself as split-second, tactical knowledge—superfast decisions as to which shot will bring one's opponent into a position of vulnerability, when to go for the outright winner, whether to try a passing shot instead of a topspin lob—combined with the almost automatic ability to carry out these decisions rapidly and unerringly.

Unfortunately, many players who could be creative do not want to be. They are afraid of the idea. Creativity is not for them.

What's wrong with creativity? Absolutely nothing. Like its motivator, aggression, creativity is a misconstrued concept. But whereas the popular conception of aggression is half right, that of creativity is quite wrong. Creativity has been imbued with a mystical quality it does not possess. It has been assigned as the province of a chosen few, and has been suffused with a kind of elitist eccentricity which is totally misconceived.

Cop-Outs from Creativity

Two inhibiting myths have grown up around the idea of creativity.

· Myth #1 : *Creativity is born of inspiration, a sudden illumination, something out of nowhere.*

This is not only wishful thinking, it is a wonderful cop-out. It allows those pubescents and postpubescents who "know" they are "unique" and "meant" for something "special" to sit around waiting for it to happen until they can neither know nor mean much, anymore—at which time they usually moan a lot about having been "passed by." Worse still, it allows the rest of us who (secretly) recognize ourselves to be rather ordinary types to keep on seeing, feeling, and doing things in the same old boring, constricted, everyday sort of way, never even trying to be creative beyond the obligatory fling or two at flaming crepes, newspaper collages, and lopsided ceramics.

Although sudden illuminations do occur, and the solutions to nonsituationally creative problems have sometimes come by way of dreams, or after a period of sleep or diversion, creativity is rarely born of inspiration. In actuality, inspiration is the result of using ordinary thought processes in a unique way for the purpose of attaining an ordinary goal. Inspiration is a very quick step in what, in most cases, is a rather lengthy and difficult process.

Because much of the work involved in this step is not done at the conscious level of thought, illumination or inspiration may look and feel like something much more unusual than it is. Because it looks and feels different—seems to differ from the rote, associative, and trial-and-error thought/behavior patterns ordinarily used in everyday life—this "unique" way of thinking and doing can seem to be mystical. But, it never is.

· Myth #2: *With few exceptions, all genuinely creative people are "geniuses," and all geniuses are, by definition, both mystically "gifted" and a little crazy.*

This too is both wishful thinking and a cop-out. A prime reason why most people make no attempt at creativity is that they are terrified of both self-actualization and failure. They therefore remove themselves from the possibility of being creative by deeming those who forge ahead "geniuses"—deformed, eccentric, or crazy. For while it is quite all right in this psychiatrically enlightened age to have a neurotic for a neighbor, or to take a neurotic to lunch, a psychotic not in our own image is something else again.

Many genuinely creative people have themselves fallen for the "crazy genius" myth, and frequently work to perpetuate it. Only masochists want to remember how essentially unpleasant much hard work really is. The discoverers of truly unique solutions want to forget the tedium of preparation, the grinding work of getting out and actually doing something—the sweats, the cramps, the aches, the anxiety, the insomnia; the bouts of panic, fury, and self-doubt that go into the conception and completion of any new piece of work which, no matter how good, may fail in a world where results are all that really count. Magic is much easier, though more fleeting. And if one is not a consistent winner, isn't it better to be seen as a crazy part-time genius than as a consistently driven drudge?

Moreover, since much of the work leading to inspiration is unconscious, the actual process is often difficult to explain, even to oneself. It can very easily seem to the winner/drudge that the winning thing did almost come from nowhere. Although it never does.

The Creative Process

Creativity is goal-directed thought/behavior. Any creative endeavor has one of two goals: to find a new solution to an existing problem, or to find a new way of expressing an idea or concept. Situational creativity—the type of creativity involved in tennis—is directed toward a fast, pragmatic version of the first goal. It aims to achieve a successful solution to a problem existing at the moment.

The creative process is composed of four steps: preparation, incubation, illumination, and verification.

Preparation involves study of the work of others, instruction, and self-instruction, including self-training and practice. In terms of thought/behavior processes, most preparation involves rote, associative and trial-and-error learning, and the setting into long-term memory of this information. In tennis, preparation requires the repetition of overhead after overhead, backhand after backhand—correctly done, of course. The result is the deposit of proprioceptive knowledge in the long-term memory bank.

The second step, incubation, primarily involves the concentrated execution of the first three steps of analytic thought: inspecting, listing, and weighing. Selection of applicable segments of the work of others and of one's own previous efforts takes place here. These segments, which constitute one's alternatives, are then mentally weighed as to the relative importance of each. This, as previously noted, is the process of optimization.

Illumination, which is sometimes called "inspiration," is the probability-based selection of the most promising alternative. This third step is the cortical "magic." It does not take place on a conscious level. Rather, the tennis player's brain responds on a subcognitive level in selecting how and where he should hit the next return.

Verification, the fourth and final step, is a trial-and-error activity. This is where the risk which most people fear occurs. You put to the test the alternative which your cortex has selected as the most workable. You try it out. In tennis, if it works, you are that much closer to winning. If it fails, you had better do something about it after the game—such as going back to step 1 and thinking more with sensations and less with words.

In terms of duration and duress, step 1 of the creative process is long and hard, step 2 is short and hard, step 3 seems quick and easy, step 4 is quick and hard—particularly if, this time, you do not succeed.

A clear example of situational creativity within a well-planned overall strategy came in the 1975 Wimbledon finals, when Arthur Ashe used not only every psychological ploy in defeating Jimmy Connors, but a creative array of shots as well. Connors had just beaten Roscoe Tanner of the 140-mile-an-hour serve in the semifinals, and was all prepared to rifle back Ashe's searing serves and backhand drives. Ashe hit instead a variety of slices, drop shots, and lobs mixed in with occasional whistling backhand drives to keep Connors off balance. It was as if Ashe instinctively selected the ideal shot on every return.

Creative People

Research concerning the personality characteristics of creative individuals reveals that they usually possess such traits as independence, dominance, flexibility, and freedom from preconception. As with all winning players, their need to establish identity is very strong, as is their desire to possess the situation rather than be possessed by it.

Where creative people differ from all but the truly great tennis players is in degree of motivation and type of perception. Creative individuals are extremely highly motivated toward reaching their goal through problem-solving. And being so, they continue to utilize a technique which the average person shuts down somewhere toward the end of childhood—an openness, a willingness to search out and try new alternatives. Like the truly great tennis players, those creative people who produce results have a toughness which the average person is too scared and too lazy to develop. They condition themselves, with the aid of motivation, to be tough enough to take failure and keep on going—to get up, go back, reassess, rework, and get on with it.

Their need to achieve their goal—and, ultimately, to enhance their realization of identity—works to widen the perception of creative people. It could be said that their angle of vision is often somewhat askew. They will not learn to narrow it. They look at things from angles the existence of which most people are trained (and, in turn, train themselves) not to envision. In step 2 of the creative process—incubation—they do not exclude alternatives which most other people would consider inapplicable.

Intelligence is apparently unrelated to any type or degree of tennis ability. Although they are quick to point out certain exceptions, even the world-class players hold this belief, and tennis teaching pros are in accord. Several research investigations reported in *The Research Quarterly* and other journals have confirmed the hypothesis that tennis ability and intelligence are mutually independent.

In one study, no statistically significant correlation could be found between intelligence and ability at either tennis or badminton. Another study found no relationship between general physical skill and intellectual levels in a college population. Still another showed no correlation between intelligence and motor skills in children.

As we noted in the section on memory/practice, there may be a qualitative difference between the flexible, creative brain and the more rigid one. There may possibly be a difference in the quality and rapidity of function at the synapse. This is only a theory, however, and concrete proof is not yet available.

In sum, creativity plays its major role in tennis in the many decisions governed by the immediate court situation. It is, for the most part, a matter of tactics. The player with the best tactical game is likely to be the one with a great variety of strokes and patterns of play at his immediate command. He has completed step 1 long before he sets foot on the court for any particular match. He knows his strokes and patterns, and has used them frequently in highly motivated play. As a consequence, his brain has a rich complex of engrams from which to draw. Providing that he is sufficiently motivated, his cortex will proceed to coordinate particularly intricate and novel combinations of engrams appropriate to overcoming the situation at hand—if he concentrates sufficiently to allow his motivated cortex to effectively do its intended work.

CHAPTER SEVEN

Warmup

THERE are two aspects to the warmup: assessment and readiness. Both psychology and physiology are involved. The purpose of the warmup is the attainment of an internal psychophysiological state adequate for the type and degree of competitive activity that tennis involves.

Exercise and "Mental Practice"

From a physiological standpoint, the warmup should represent a gradual transition from rest to activity. It will not only aid performance but also prevent muscle tears. It has been hypothesized that warmups decrease internal muscle viscosity and resistance, thus allowing a more rapid and forceful contraction.

Since each player has a different optimal warmup time, exercises must be custom designed. A good rule of thumb is to exercise until the circulation to the muscles is improved.

A slight glow should be felt. Stretching exercises should be included, but in order to prevent a rebound contraction, these should be mild. Walking at a brisk pace, jogging, and stretching are a good beginning.

In order to fine-tune patterns of coordination, balance, and timing, additional time and more closely focused concentration are necessary. Here it is important to duplicate the movements involved in the event itself. Even the weight of the racket should be the same as in the game situation.

One of the most important results of this type of careful run-through is the reinforcement of kinesthetic memory, specifically a reactivation of pertinent engrams. This can be done through "mental practice." This involves "visualizing," a somewhat unconventional way of bringing information into the long-term memory bank of motor function by thinking, "seeing," and mentally "feeling" the motion of a particular tennis stroke.

The theory is that thinking will duplicate the electrical activity which takes place in the brain during actual physical movement, albeit at a lower intensity than during the game situation. This technique is not superior to actual practice, nor does it improve muscle strength or cardiovascular fitness. It has only to do with neuromuscular coordination.

There are two basic prerequisites to mental practice: (1) the player must know how to perform the stroke correctly, and (2) he must possess some ability to visualize such physical movement. If one knows how to perform a stroke very well and can focus one's concentration, shutting out all distraction, it is easy to visualize it. Mental practice is best executed by the less rigid, more imaginative type of individual.

An advanced skier we know says that he improves between seasons by visualizing himself skiing down a trail, doing all the turns and jumps in his repertoire. He discovered mental practice quite by accident. While looking forward to the coming season, and putting in a bit of time daydreaming about it, he found that he could actually "feel" his weight shift to the downhill ski. When it finally snowed and the grand first day arrived, he skied better than the last day of the previous season. And all that season, he did well on those impossible slopes which had given him a bit of trouble the previous year.

One aspect of the game requiring both physical and mental warmup is strategy. To begin the match dependent only on one's strokes and wits is to be about one-third prepared. Even though strategy can never be worked out to the nth degree before a match, an overall plan should be thought out and its basics both mentally and physically worked through. This will both provide some focus for fine-tuning and help to achieve a state of cortical readiness.

Assessment

The *psychological aspects* of warmup center around assessment and arousal. Of these, assessment comes first.

Different players tend to react to the same stimulus in different ways, and will sometimes react in a manner contrary to what the opponent expects. Additionally, from one time to another, all players will tend to vary significantly in their motivation and applied ability.

Rick, a strong amateur player, says, "I always think of warmup as 'size-up time.' You look over the situation. You try to measure everything you're going to be up against. Which can be tricky, because you, yourself, are trying to look as dumb and stupid as you can, so as not to give anything away. So, you play them like they were all like a bunch of hungry mice. Tease them with that little piece of cheese that they can't keep. Drop short, and see what they do. Play real nice, and see what happens. Do something stupid. See how they react. You'll find, yourself, that it's good training. Because, you never know, he may be doing the same thing to you."

Court Personality

Once on court, many players tend to change, to take on a "court personality" which may be totally different from the way they are in "real" life. A player may become rock steady or nervous; he may have to become frightened or angry before he seriously starts to play; or he may have a short-fused temper and become surprisingly hostile. Or he may suddenly exhibit a surprising need to perform for the spectators.

A player's court personality may contain no elements of what is best about him or her, and it is almost sure to include some of the worst. Whatever it may be, that is the personality which must be played against—the personality of the moment—and not the one which may be displayed either before or after the match.

Because of this, it is best to assess the opponent's court personality on-site where it counts most, to be as observant and objective as possible, and to consciously try to determine the type of game which will least cater to it. Inevitably, as play progresses and fatigue comes closer and closer, the negatives displayed in the course of warmup will be accentuated.

Ilie Nastase becomes a flamboyant, uninhibited showman on the court. He will quick-serve his opponent. He will delay the match. He is often the victim of his own tactics, becoming so agitated in his act that his tennis proceeds to suffer. He has created a tragicomic on-court character, and seems to have become his own creation. Off the court he is witty, even charming, insisting that he is not a wicked person, that he just plays mean tennis. A few days after the Stockholm match in which Arthur Ashe walked off the court because of Nastase's behavior, he gave Ashe a bouquet of flowers, contending that he really did like Ashe, that Ashe was a nice guy even if he had walked off the court.

Ille Nastase displays his objection to a lineman's call.

When he is good—playing straight, serious tennis—he can show brilliance in his play. But it seems that that happens only when it has to. On his best behavior, when he faced possible suspension as a result of his actions in a tournament two weeks before, he beat Raul Ramirez in a thrilling match in the 1975 U.S. Open. After his victory, he could not believe himself: "For me, it is fantastic to behave like this."

The "unreality" of the game allows an individual to drop the inhibitions of everyday life and become his "real" self. Court personality is not a constant. From one situation to another, much of what will be displayed depends on the player's attitude toward his opponent and how capable he considers himself of playing a respectable game against him.

Rick comments on the psyching-out qualities of one of the more effective "put-ons" of court personality: "What I do when I'm out there is I see to it that I look like I have no more personality than your average machine that is out to beat down, wear out, and grind up whatever happens to be on the other side of that net. They seem to expect something that acts more human. It gets to a lot of people."

How much of court personality is situation-determined is open to question. In 1968, Walter Mischel, a social scientist of the behaviorist school, argued that there was not more than a 20 to 30 percent correlation between personality traits and general behavior. He contended that situational factors are the major determinants of behavior, and that personality traits evoke consistent behavior only when the individual is in similar environmental situations and where the important stimuli are the same. A rather lively intradisciplinary quarrel erupted with the publication of Mischel's work, and it has not been resolved to this day. Most authorities accept a combined situation-trait approach to personality theory.

Tennis Personality

Whatever is displayed on court will in all probability contain some aspects of that core of personality characteristics which are essentially those of the high achiever.

Individuals who are strongly motivated to achieve are determined, driven, and egocentric, and have an internalized standard of excellence. Their motivation is intrinsic: they set their own goals, psych themselves up, and go about achieving them on their own. They need no one to tell them what they have to do, or why they have to do it. They have strong desires for dominance. They can sometimes be quite daring. They are able to resist social pressure. They will work hard and well at tasks where the odds are not in their favor. They are competitive; they are aggressive; they are basically loners. One of the four championship qualities listed by Billie Jean King is that the athlete must hate to lose; and Pancho Segura is equally emphatic about this.

Billie Jean King, an aggressive competitor, vents her frustration on a tennis ball after missing a shot.

Singles has always been thought the province of the individual achiever—the player who is both achievement-oriented and self-oriented. Even in his early days as a tennis promoter, Bobby Riggs said that every champion, from Tilden through Gonzales, liked to see his name in bold-letter headlines. Carole Caldwell Graebner, for many years one of the top-ten women players, says that tennis players are selfish, sometimes arrogant people. She states categorically, "Everyone in tennis is out for himself!" Even college tennis players show little cooperative spirit. This is in contrast to participants in other college sports, where it is almost universal for an upperclassman to take a freshman under his wing. (The system of ranking players by ability no doubt contributes to this intra-team competitiveness.)

Apparent exceptions to aggressiveness are evident at all

levels of tennis. Despite the many players he had ground into the clay, Guillermo Vilas is mild-mannered, poetry loving, personally shy and self-effacing. On the court, he is noted for his steadiness, and although strong at volleying, he rarely rushes the net. He describes himself as always being nervous before a match.

Our friend Marty Sher remembers the number-one man on his college team as exhibiting quiet self-confidence both on and off court. He was unaggressive in his off-court interpersonal relationships, but on court his win-loss record was phenomenal. He almost never made unforced errors—everything was returned. He almost never hit aces or spectacular winners. His ego strength was evident in that he was not bothered by heckling; he would delight in subtly causing frustrations for his opponents. Interestingly, on the day after graduation, he sold both his rackets for a total of ten dollars and quit tennis.

Arousal

Going purely by "looseness" and gut feeling, the player must write the prescription for attaining his optimal degree of arousal. A continuing controversy exists as to whether the energized individual performs better or worse than one who enters physical competition in a state of reduced tension.

Psyching Up

Some psychologists contend that performance level is directly correlated with the athlete's degree of anxiety. Others hold to the Yerkes-Dodson law, which states that up to a given point, anxiety will increase performance, but that additional anxiety will be progressively detrimental to performance. One study of college football players showed that a large fluctuation in pregame anxiety levels was the factor which most impaired performance. The same study found that a steady increase from low to moderate anxiety levels on the day of the game coincided with best performance. Finally, two studies of wrestling and crew found that the most successful athletes in these sports exhibited low levels of "in-competition" (or state) anxiety.

The best conclusion which can be drawn is that raising precompetition arousal must be done with caution, if at all, and that such psychological strategy must be highly individualized. Observation of professional tennis players seems to bear this out. There is a wide range of temperaments. A few names from the top illustrate the degree of variation: Vilas, Connors, Nastase, Ashe, Borg, Panatta, Newcombe. Some are frequently nervous before a tournament match, others occasionally so.

Anger has a facilitating influence on some players; as a rule, these are often highly competitive, sometimes hostile personalities. Alan King, one of the most competitive players among the celebrities, says he has a special technique for psyching himself up: visualizing everyone on the other side of the net as a television network vice-president. When Rosemary Casals' anger rises, the quality of her tennis can swiftly follow. In the early days of World Team Tennis, while playing Pam Teeguarden (then of the Sets) and behind 3–0, she heard a Sets fan shout, "Rosie who?" Furious, Casals won six of the next seven games. Anger also improves Jimmy Connors' game. When the fans are against him, he wants to hit every shot for a winner "just to make them mad." And he often does both.

On the other hand, an incident from basketball illustrates the possible counterproductive effects of heightened arousal. Interviewed by the press the day before he was to face his former team, the Seattle SuperSonics, Knicks player Spencer Haywood detailed a number of grievances against his old team. He then proceeded to work himself up into such a state of intense hostility that he played at his very worst, scoring only six points the entire game.

Psyching Down

Most recreational players have trouble suppressing anxiety. One of their major warmup problems is how to psych down.

Some people go to sleep. The great soccer star Pelé is often fast asleep with a towel over his head before a game. He must be awakened by his teammates when it is time to take to the soccer field.

Some people exercise. Tests have shown that regular exercise can have the effect of reducing anxiety. In a recent study investigating the effects of exercise deprivation, subjects were selected whose routine daily activity included moderate to strenuous exercise of a noncompetitive nature. They were deprived of exercise for one month. At the end of that time, the subjects exhibited increased sexual tension, increased need to be with others, and increased general levels of anxiety.

Vigorous exercise can reduce state anxiety. In some individuals, the reduction begins following the exercise period. In most others, it begins with the initiation of exercise and continues thereafter. In all cases, anxiety levels continue to decline for thirty minutes or more following the exercise period.

There are three basic psychological methods for reducing anxiety. Of these, the first two can easily be utilized in the warmup period : (1) combined relaxation and desensitization, and (2) diversion of attention, or the employment of substitute activity. The third method, traditional psychotherapy, uses reflection, clarification, and interpretation to help the individual gain insight into the underlying causes of anxiety. When these three methods were tested on a sample of college students, relaxation-desensitization proved the most generally successful although the other two methods also succeeded to varying degrees.

Entering more tournaments and successively more difficult ones will usually result in a gradual reduction of environment-induced anxiety. It will also acclimatize the player to a variety of courts other than his home court. The degree of anxiety produced by playing before spectators can also be reduced by desensitization. If one's sensibilities are especially reactive, start with one spectator, a friend. It may be helpful to know that it is an almost universal trait, when performing before spectators, to want to dig a hole, jump in, and make yourself invisible. Tennis players are by no means alone in these desires. They also occur among artists, surgeons, teachers, and classical musicians.

Social and psychophysiological self-distractions are also helpful in preventing excessive anxiety. Avoid a long period of waiting for the match to go on. Most importantly, do not wait around alone. It is usually best either to occupy oneself elsewhere, and not show up earlier than necessary for warmup, or to socialize with the other players.

Relaxation for Concentration

Although at first glance concentration and relaxation would seem to be at odds, careful observation will reveal the two qualities to be synergistic rather than competitive. Concentration can be used to bring about a relaxed state, and relaxation used to improve concentration. The idea is to make effort effortless. Timothy Gallwey, author of *The Inner Game of Tennis,* not only agrees with this idea but also adds an aesthetic touch. He looks for beauty in the arc of flight and in the crescents of light and shade on the ball, and he finds that such concentration leads to relaxation and a completely free swing.

Because psychiatry and medicine have long recognized the

health-threatening effects of stress and anxiety, various relaxation techniques have been recommended over the years as preventive therapy.

Most of these techniques involve the following steps. First, do not allow yourself to feel any sense of guilt for taking the fifteen or twenty minutes of time out for relaxation. Psych yourself up for the beneficial effects of relaxation. Next, assume a comfortable position. Third, tense or stretch the muscles of your body and then relax them. Finally, concentrate on breathing or on a single word, such as "quiet," "relax," or "serene."

Whether relaxation helps athletic performance may be open to question, but there is no contesting its longevity value for Donal McLaughlin. Quoted in a *New York Times* article in December 1975, he said, "I never exerted myself with too much work or ambition." He is now working on his second hundred years.

Meditation, Anyone?

A special and much publicized relaxation technique is meditation, which came into vogue in the United States in the late 1960s. Its chief popularizer, Maharishi Mahesh Yogi, modified the mental and physical rigors of the Oriental practices, so that even soft and self-indulgent Americans could "meditate." Then the Maharishi's brand of transcendental meditation (TM) gained great numbers of adherents. The phenomenon soon aroused the interest of physiologists as well as social scientists. Their research results seem to point to the generalization that a little meditation never hurt anyone, if only as a sanctioned method by which to engage in guilt-free relaxation. Individuals who meditate considerably more than the recommended twice daily may be subject to hallucinations, however.

Robert Keith Wallace at the University of California and Herbert Benson at Harvard found that meditation resulted in a marked reduction in metabolic rate, as measured by oxygen consumption. Two results which correlate with a state of reduced anxiety were also achieved: a reduction in blood lactate concentration and an increase in electrical resistance of the skin. Following the measurement of many other parameters, the overall conclusion was that the meditative state was one of physiologic relaxation.

There also seemed to be a residual benefit once the meditation period was over and bodily function returned to normal levels. For example, in subjects with hypertension, meditation on a regular basis reportedly brought about a long-term lowering of blood pressure.

The degree to which meditation affects psychological function and physical performance has also been investigated. A number of factors important to athletic performance, such as concentration, perceptual ability, reaction time, endurance, and running speed, have been included in these investigations. Some of the results show meditation to be somewhat beneficial, but others are too marginal to be significant. Nor do the performance records of world-class athletes who meditate show with certainty that meditation is effective in sports.

Throughout history, in both the East and the West, the meditative state has been recognized as an established and well-defined type of focused awareness. All the major religions have provided for its attainment infrequently by the many and more frequently by the elect. From feelings of oneness, through the various facets of grace, to visitations by the miraculous, all the major religions can supply numerous recorded instances of those who attained such states.

With practice—and with or without a sound-thought amulet, such as the mantras and special training prescribed by the TM folk—any individual should be able to enter the meditative (or hypometabolic) state. The requirements are closely akin to those for other relaxation techniques. Meditative concentration should be passive. You should first allow the mind to become devoid of all peripheral, potentially intervening throughts and images. Then, after assuming a comfortable position in a quiet environment, you can proceed to focus concentration on breathing or on a word.

How About a Drink?

In submaximal exercise in the upright position (e.g., tennis), alcohol reduces all parameters of cardiovascular function. The same work load requires a higher heart rate and greater oxygen consumption. At very high blood alcohol levels (200 mg/100ml = 6 double shots of Scotch), there is a direct toxic effect on the heart muscle.

At only three double shots, there is no apparent evidence of toxicity, even though some rather absurdly nonproductive changes tend to occur in brain function and, hence, in the effectiveness of one's game.

Sex and the Singles Player

On few issues is there such controversy as on whether sex and tennis make a sound mix.

Psychological Factors

Distinct differences appear to exist between male and female perceptions of the effects of sexual activity on athletic performance in general, and on tennis in particular.

Of the women tennis players interviewed, virtually all, from novice to professional, reported no direct adverse effects on their game. Most said that they had never thought of sex in connection with tennis and concluded that, if there was any influence, it could not have escaped their notice. Some commented that sex the night before a match made them more relaxed and contributed to a generally more positive outlook. Only one woman reported any loss of concentration (and an occasional loss of points) because of daydreaming about the night before.

Among males, the perceived influence of sex on tennis varies from benign to malevolent. Some reported that sexual activity within twenty-four hours of a match had no noticeable influence on their game. Others discerned distinct effects on the musculoskeletal system, reporting that their legs "felt like rubber" the next day. The quadriceps—the muscle group of the front of the thigh—seemed particularly affected. One of the male pros reported a three-day delay in adverse effects.

Several sports are guided by the tradition that sex is detrimental to the male athlete's performance. Football generally has a "four day" rule. The Miami Dolphins are reported to place their players in virtual detainment for two days before an important game. The Oriental martial arts, such as karate, judo, and aikido, prescribe an abstinence period of considerable duration. In preparation for a tournament, for example, a high-degree black belt holder will abstain for at least two weeks. Some of the old masters will shun women for six months. Karate instructors contend that they can tell which of their male students have had sexual intercourse the day before by the diminished height of their kick.

Humans have a tendency either to belittle or deify what they cannot possess. It might follow that, regardless of gender, the less sexually well-adjusted one is, the more vocal one may be in denigrating the positive effects of what cannot help but be a conflict-laden area of activity. Many impotent men passionately involve themselves in substitute activity—frequently, in some form of athletics. This attitude may even extend to the arts. Vincent Van Gogh held that, in order to allow his art to come alive, the male artist should be abstinent. This opinion is quite in line with middle-class Victorian literature, as well as the reported beliefs of some primitive societies, some ancient civilizations, some mystics, some psychotics, some rather average adolescent males, and some of their parents. But that does not make it true.

Lawrence Morehouse, a California exercise physiologist, is viewed by the athletic establishment as a radical. Morehouse feels that athletes do *better* after sex, even the morning of competition, and advises coaches to encourage their athletes to bring their mates along on the "away" games and meets. The fact is that although both strenuous physical activity and severe emotional stress tend to inhibit sexual activity, moderate physical activity, combined with a sense of well-being, seems to be one of the better stimuli. Many tennis players note that sexual activity increases when they are playing regularly and are in good condition.

Nevertheless, unless one is engaging in sex for the specific purpose of relieving an uncomfortable degree of tension, sexual activity can diminish one's focused concentration. Once in bed with an attractive partner, the average tennis player may experience some difficulty in remaining really psyched up about tomorrow's or this afternoon's game.

Sex is a means of ego enhancement, satisfying such ego needs as recognition, achievement, dominance, and autonomy. This means that satisfactory sex before the game may cause the player to behave less aggressively, and unsatisfactory sex may have the opposite effect. But it can also mean that satisfactory sex before the game will cause the now ego-enhanced player to feel more confident. Having reached the first rung on the ladder of winning, he or she may feel better equipped to strive for the achievement of the next "conquest" on the court. Conversely, unsatisfactory sex, with its inevitable depletion of ego, may cause the player to take either of two paths: to strive for compensatory excellence and behave more aggressively, so as to achieve a substitute goal; or to accede to this feeling of ego depletion by behaving less aggressively and less creatively. Since individual reactions can vary so greatly, no general advice can be given.

Psychophysiological Factors

Numerous research studies have been conducted on the physiological effects of sexual intercourse upon the human body. The physiological data show a less than narrow range of consistency. The bias effect of uniformly small samples—until recently, one of the prime criticisms—no longer holds sway, since more recent studies have utilized large samples of subjects. But although recent samples have also been carefully screened, the very nature of this type of research precludes the possibility of achieving the absolute randomness and objectivity necessary for unbiased results.

Other criticisms are even more far-reaching. To our knowledge, none of these studies has detailed the influence of such psychological basics as the subject's emotional set, attitude toward partner, degree of intensity of their emotional bond, or frequency and recency of sexual activity prior to the experiment. The majority of physiological research has been directed toward determining the effects of sexual activity on the cardiovascular and respiratory systems. There has been less investigation of its effects on the musculoskeletal and central nervous systems—systems which are, in their own way, as critical to sex as they are to tennis.

Research findings on the physiological aspects of sexual activity agree that increases in heart rate, blood pressure, respiration, oxygen consumption, and muscular contraction occur during intercourse. However, some discrepancy exists between the quantitative values reported from study to study.

The trend in findings has been to decrease the recorded amount of physiological exertion involved in sex. For example, an early study recorded pulse rates of close to 170 per minute and respiratory rates above 60 per minute. Both values are equivalent to those of moderately strenuous athletic activity—for example, a couple of brisk sets. Recorded pulse and respiratory rates are now more closely the equivalents of those attained in the course of a brisk walk or a period of emotional stress at work.

One large study indicated wide variations in physiologic response, with pulse rates at and just preceding orgasm ranging from 100 to 180 per minute, and systolic blood pressure elevations of from 40 to 100 mm of mercury above normal for males, and from 30 to 80 above for females. Respiratory rates were up to 40 per minute for both sexes. In males, respiration rapidly returned to normal after orgasm. In females, hyperventilation at maximum rates would sometimes continue until attainment of additional orgasms. In addition to those of the primary sex organs, muscle contractions (myotonia) were exhibited for both sexes in the arms, legs, trunk, neck, and face. Intense contraction of the hands and feet (carpopedal spasm) was a frequent finding in both sexes.

More recent studies have found markedly lower values. The figures for heart rate at orgasm have averaged less than 120 per minute, the oxygen intake averaged 60 percent of maximal. Perhaps this is one way in which science mirrors life. As societal attitudes toward heterosexual activity become more casual, so do those of the subjects of research studies. Hence, the intensity of their monitored activities declines.

Before we leave this topic, we must note two bits of scientific evidence which conflict with the traditional hypothesis of an antagonism between sex and athletics, and which point instead to a connection between sexual activity and strength enhancement. First, during athletic training, muscle size and strength increase to a greater extent under the influence of testosterone-like drugs. Second, endogenous testosterone is increased during periods of sexual activity. Coaches prescribing frequent sexual activity during training might then be on solid theoretical ground. For now, however, we must await future scientific studies and actual scoreboard results before being able to draw firm conclusions.

Coping with the Environment

Both in warmup and in-game, the player must compensate for various environmental influences.

Heat and Humidity

The body's efficiency as a work-producing machine is considerably less than 100 percent. Muscle contraction produces a lot of energy which is not transformed into work. This unused energy produces heat which must be dissipated if the player's body temperature is to remain at normal and the possibility of heat stroke is to be avoided. The rapidity of heat dissipation depends on the temperature-humidity index and how fast the player is burning calories.

The constancy of body temperature is normally maintained by the circulatory system. If the difference between environmental temperature and body temperature is sufficient, whatever excess body heat is generated by mild to moderate exercise will be brought to the surface by blood flow to the skin, where it can leave by conduction, convection, and radiation. The closer the environmental temperature gets to 98.6°F, however, the less adequate blood flow becomes as a dissipater of excess body heat. Cooling is then accomplished primarily by the evaporation of sweat. The higher the humidity, the slower the evaporation of sweat and the greater the danger of a rise in body temperature.

High environmental temperature produces an increase in heart rate, a decrease in stroke volume, and in some cases a decrease in diastolic blood pressure. There is a consequent decrease in work capacity: the body attempts to see to it that the player stops trying to burn calories fast.

Sweating can produce sufficient fluid loss to cause dehydration and impairment of performance. Unless the fluid loss reaches extraordinary proportions, however, maximal oxygen uptake will not be affected, although total work capacity will be.

Some physiologists advise as much as eight ounces of water every half hour for anyone exercising in a hot, dry environment. Tennis affords many opportunities to stop for a few ounces of water (changing sides every other game and between sets), and the water is quickly absorbed from the gastrointestinal tract into the bloodstream. As the proverbial grandmothers used to say, "It wouldn't hurt."

Altitude

If the average North American recreational player should happen to go to Mexico City and attempt to play tennis shortly after arrival, he will experience marked shortness of breath and a much decreased capacity to move fast and hit hard. He will tire quickly. Hopefully, he will slow down voluntarily, before his oxygen transport system forces him to.

The reason for his difficulty is that his body, accustomed to functioning at sea level or a few hundred feet above, will suddenly find itself with less oxygen to work with. It will move more slowly. Work capacity will be diminished. The heart will have to work harder in order to meet even the normal demands of the nonacclimatized body.

Here is the physiological explanation: When oxygen pressure is lower in the blood than in the lungs, oxygen leaves the lungs and enters the blood plasma; and when oxygen pressure is lower in the muscles than in the plasma, it leaves the plasma, enters the muscles, and keeps them working. The higher the altitude, the lower the air pressure; and, consequently, the lower the pressure of oxygen within the body.

At the end of two weeks, the player will find his game somewhat improved. He will now be playing at fully one-half his normal, lower-altitude efficiency. Full acclimatization will come, but it is a slow process, taking longer than the time span of the average vacation.

The moral of this is: play in your own backyard. If your racket compels you to take it along on vacation, either acclimatize first and play later, or seek your own level.

CHAPTER EIGHT

In-Game

THE psychological and psychophysiological information necessary for actual play has been presented in the previous chapters. It is now up to the player to use this information to formulate a strategy tailored to his or her individual skills and needs.

Play the Percentages

There are many rules of strategy which the singles player should make part of his game.

Match your pace to the playing surface. On clay, don't rush the net on a mediocre preparatory shot, and don't try for a put-away from the baseline when your opponent is at his baseline.

- From a corner backcourt position, it is better to approach the net behind a shot down the line than following a cross-court shot.
- Don't hit the first serve so hard that it has less than a 50 percent chance of being good.

The list goes on and on, filling any number of instruction books. The point is that for anyone of less than world-class caliber, percentage tennis is synonymous with winning. The shot that has a margin of safety should be used in preference to the one that does not.

Risk should be reduced to a minimum. Let your opponent make the errors. If given the chance, most recreational players will hit unforced errors. If given the chance, most of them will faithfully lose the game.

You don't need winners to win. You need only get the ball into the opponent's court with consistency and a *little* something on it. Your shots should clear the net by three feet, and should land with a minimum six-foot margin from the baseline.

Resist the urge to make a lot of little squares of fuzz and rubber out of the ball. Where a soft, sure shot will win the point, do not go for the smash. "Putting the ball away" connotes place, not velocity.

Roy Emerson, who holds titles by the dozens, stresses percentage tennis in his teaching. He advises the player with a weak backhand to take advantage of the middle of the net, six inches lower than the ends, by hitting that backhand shot cross-court instead of down the line.

A general percentage rule-of-thumb advises that when you are at the baseline, hit cross-court; when at midcourt, hit down the middle; and when at the net, hit cross-court, again. The cross-court return of service, and even the cross-court slice as an approach shot, are considered by many as percentage shots.

Of course, these percentage rules are subject to modification by the opponent's position, and both the opponent's and the player's specific strengths and weaknesses. The element of surprise is occasionally worth a violation of the percentages. But, most often, it is the percentage that pays off—not the exceptions.

The top professionals are the only players who may occasionally scoff at the percentage shot and successfully go for a difficult winner. Their guided-missile accuracy permits it. But even they must rely on percentage play for the greater part of their game. In the 1977 Grand Slam finals, for example, Bjorn Borg took the measure of Jimmy Connors. Borg patiently kept the pressure on Connors from the baseline, varying his shots but hitting them all with an adequate margin for error. Connors made the mistakes.

Apply Psychology

Pertinent aspects of psychology can be applied in order to influence your opponent's game. Primary among these are distortion, distraction, acclimatization, and continual variation. A fifth factor is the determination of which points or games during a match are most crucial to you and your opponent.

If these psychological factors are to be of use, they must be studied, kept in the forefront of consciousness, and constantly applied. Billie Jean King lists one of the four characteristics of winning tennis as thinking about tennis all the time, even off court. Billie Jean King is right.

Utilization of these solid psychological weapons is well within the rules and bounds of sportsmanship. Just as it is perfectly proper during warmup to take note of the sun, the wind, and the court surface, and to assess the strengths and weaknesses of the opponent's game and emotional makeup, it is also perfectly proper during the game to exploit the opponent's emotional state and to use every bit of what one has learned of psychological theory to best advantage.

Distortion

The size or apparent strength of your swing will influence your opponent's perception of the speed of the ball. This type of distortion can be effective in several ways.

A large, hefty motion for a drop shot is deceptive, while a murderous motion for an overhead may cause the opponent at the net to duck in self-protection. You then can drop the ball nicely in the middle of the court for a winner. (If you really had tried to murder it, you probably would have hit it into the net.)

The reverse is also true. A smooth, effortless motion can propel the ball faster than the law of conservation of energy would seem to allow. It will often catch your opponent thinking that he has another second to rest before starting after the ball. So artful a stroke—which takes a good deal of drill work on your part—has two requisites: it must have good form, and it must result in hitting the ball with the central area of the strings, which provides maximum power.

Distraction

Feinting is a distraction technique used by many good players. One of its prime purposes is the destruction of the opponent's concentration, distracting him from his decision as to where to hit the ball. Indecision at the moment the ball is hit always results in a weak shot, at best. The extreme example is the novice who, at the instant the ball must be hit, has not yet decided whether to hit it forehand or backhand. He often ends up hitting it with his ribs, or worse. Moreover, feinting can sometimes tempt an opponent to try and fail at a too-difficult shot.

Some decisions as to which distractive technique to use can be based on knowledge of the opponent's psychological makeup. Marty Riessen has observed, for example, that when Ilie Nastase is deprived of a little of his exhibitionism, he can neither concentrate nor bring his remarkable ability into play. Therefore, against Nastase, Riessen tries to play a dull, monotonous game—staying in the backcourt, hitting low, medium-pace shots, and generally trying to make the match as uninteresting as he can. Although we have not seen anyone attempt it, it might be equally effective to abet Nastase's tendency to become emotionally distraught. Once his arousal level is higher than optimum, his game suffers.

Not all forms of distraction are equally cricket. Taking a practice swing as your opponent is tossing the ball up to serve constitutes unacceptable distraction. While your opponent is in his service motion, it is unacceptable to do much at all. Just before the ball is in play, you may not distract him by whistling shrilly, waving your racket at him, or yelling "mine."

Moving into advantageous position after the ball is in play is an acceptable distraction, however. It is perfectly legal and ethical to break for the net just before your opponent strikes the ball. Such a motion—especially if you run like a rhino—can cause indecision, anxiety, and failure to watch the ball.

Acclimatization

Using acclimatization involves repetition followed by sudden change. For example, hit two or three deep with good pace, alternating right side and left. Then, when your opponent expects the next one to be deep and strong, slip him a drop shot or a short cross-court slice.

Acclimatization to spin has potential, too. Topspin drives can be hit to the same area of the opponent's court, two or three times in a row. These can be followed with a slice, at the same pace and place. The opponent will probably net the return.

Continual Variation

Direction, height, speed, depth, and spin can all be placed in the service of this tactic.

Continual variation can even defeat a champion. Jimmy Connors' strong returns of strong shots make it difficult to overpower him. In addition, he needs a high level of arousal for peak performance. In 1975, he lost in major tournaments to Ashe (Wimbledon), Orantes (Forest Hills), and Panatta (Stockholm). In each, he was given nothing solid to hit at. The shots against him were varied in pace, spin, and placement. There were many soft shots and many with underspin. Having to deal with so much variation prevented Connors from being able to work up his usual aggressive spirit.

Spin is especially important when your opponent is at the net, ready to volley your shot. Underspin can cause him to sink the ball right into the net.

Depth of placement can be varied to correspond with your opponent's shoelaces, wherever he may be on the court. Unless he is a soccer player, he will have trouble with such placement.

Against a player who needs a steady rhythm, the pace of play and the pace of individual strokes can be varied.

The player whose security blanket is the baseline should be brought to the net with drop shots, and then be given a chance to net a few tough overheads. Remember to lob to his backhand side.

The steady player should be given variety; but the nervous player should be treated early in the match to your best and most reliable strokes.

Crucial Points

The strategic question of crucial points and games has engendered some differences of opinion. The entire theory of crucial points is based on psychology; as such, it must be tailored to the individual player's psychophysiological strengths. Each player should examine his game and decide which point and which game are usually critical. Alternately, he might find all points are equally important to him, and that some other focus of concentration is in order.

Some players advise concentrating hardest at 30–15 and 40–30; others say 40–15 and 15–40. Arthur Ashe feels that winning the first point of any game gives a psychological advantage. Pancho Gonzales and Jimmy Connors never let up. Ken Rosewall can make a comeback from anywhere, even match point.

Exploit the Opponent's Weaknesses

There is nothing in the rules or traditions of tennis that requires one to avoid exploiting an opponent's weakness. In the early phases of the match, just as in the warmup, assess the type and degree of each weakness the opponent has. Test him on forehand, backhand, topspin, and slice. See if he can hit a low bouncing shot, and if he can take one at shoulder level or above. Can he run? Especially, can he run back from the net? Then, see to it that you utilize any advantages you can find.

No player has to be reminded to use his own strengths to advantage. But sometimes, even in the pro ranks, the player has to remind himself to play away from his opponent's strengths. Of course, you should not play every shot to weakness, or your adversary will have the warm, secure feeling of knowing where to position himself before the ball leaves your racket.

If your opponent's reaction time is slow, hit your shots early, on the rise. Do not tip him off as to where the shot is

Arthur Ashe extends his well-developed racket-arm in reaching for a difficult backhand save.

going. It is especially important not to telegraph drop shots and lobs.

Rod Laver says that you should never be embarrassed to lob. Harry Hopman says you should not be embarrassed to lob into the sun. Bobby Riggs says you should be embarrassed *not* to lob into the sun. (If, out of fairness or goodness, you fail to do so, he will think you lily-livered; and, perhaps, you should be embarrassed about that.) Do not be ashamed to let the opponent's lob bounce before hitting it.

If your opponent has a cream puff second serve, position yourself in from the baseline and use your strongest, most reliable shot to return it. This is actually a kindness. If you give him an easy return, he will probably net it anyway, and that will make him look bad. Your strong return will allow him to make a valiant effort before hitting the net. Do not feel the slightest guilt for taking full advantage—unless your second serve is more vulnerable than his.

Most recreational players have better forehands than backhands. Play to your opponent's and develop your own. Most problem backhands are related to holding back in the swing. The cure is to develop a strong wrist and grip, and then concentrate on swinging the entire arm. Forget about the flight of the ball until the swing has become free and natural; then, allow a litttle margin of safety in placement and speed. The arm–racket in motion will then do the work without its owner worrying about how to hit the shot.

When all else fails, the solution to the backhand impasse is to develop a good backhand follow-through—not a difficult task, if one eliminates the worry about hitting the ball. Then, if you miss the ball completely with your "unnatural" backhand, your follow-through will have you in perfect position to fling the racket into the backstop with your powerful and disdainful forehand.

Tips for Doubles

Singles is tennis; doubles is another sport. Doubles is small-group activity, and the dynamics which govern the success or failure of small groups govern it.

The high degree of competitiveness usually oriented toward individual performance can be channeled into a cooperative working relationship between two people. In doubles, the need to win may actually be a detriment to winning, unless it is oriented toward a win for the pair.

There are players who are strong at singles and mediocre at doubles; there are tough doubles teams whose members are weak singles players; and there are some players who win at both singles and doubles. Among the world-class players, Arthur Ashe is a solitary, self-oriented individual, superb at singles but comparatively poor at doubles. On the other hand, no less an egocentric loner than Jimmy Connors can be excellent at doubles. Billie Jean King and Rosemary Casals are aggressive in their persons and in their tennis. They win in both singles and doubles. Margaret Court is personally antithetical to both of her colleagues. She is introverted, conservative, keeps to herself, and is propriety personified. Yet both her singles and her doubles games are as strong as King's and Casals'.

A successful doubles pairing seems to be dictated by either personality or situation. Some individuals can rather easily subordinate their needs to the dictates of expediency. They may be fiercely competitive, but when the situation calls for it, they can channel their competitiveness against the enemy rather than against both the enemy and the partner. It can be conjectured that in successful doubles teams where personality is the dynamic factor, both members are less rigid than the ordinary tennis player and possess greater self-esteem. They can shift from active to passive, or from dominant to subordinate roles, without feeling threatened.

In tennis doubles, as in life, some pairs work, play, and get along better than others. The pair functions well together either because of mutual respect or an accepted dominant-subordinate relationship. Rosemary Casals admired Billie Jean King, and Billie Jean encouraged an aggressive style of play in her. Given their personalities, Jimmy Connors and Ilie Nastase would seem an unlikely doubles team; yet they have been quite successful, winning major doubles championships. When Connors was a kid, Nastase befriended him, and the two have continued to get along. Perhaps this is why, in doubles, the usually dominant, arrogant Connors plays the psychically subordinate role.

Doubles partners need not have the same personality type

Ille Nastase and Jimmy Connors in action during a men's doubles title match in 1975.

or style of play. Partners with complementary strengths often make a better team. Chris Evert provides an example. She was a notoriously average doubles player until she teamed first with Olga Morozova and then with Martina Navratilova— both strong net players. In each case, steadiness and aggressiveness were fused into a winning pair.

A University of Michigan psychologist, Alvin Zander, has done extensive work in isolating the factors making for group success or failure. A key ingredient of group success, he found, was a need for group achievement, along with an emphasis on the rewards of success. The goal of the group should be realistic; given the collective ability of its members, the group should have a realistic chance of achieving it. An increased desire for success comes from a strong sense of unity and common purpose. The trappings of group cohesion are also help-

ful: a name, a place, a common style of clothing, recognition
from outsiders, a sense of being different from other groups.
If the individuals are given some degree of responsibility relative to the group's purpose and effectiveness, team spirit will
be enhanced.

Communications

Zander found that another factor important in developing
team spirit was good communications between the members.
This is an extremely important factor in doubles play; but
doubles communication differs from that of most other
groups in that it is almost entirely nonverbal.

Doubles partners must at all times possess a mutual awareness of their respective abilities, thought processes, and position, and they must be able to plan several moves ahead. Like
the good singles player, the doubles team tries to maneuver
its opponents into a position of vulnerability and then hit for
a winner. In order to do this, the partners must share a single
tactical goal on each point or segment of the game. Since
there is no time for leisurely discussion, the language must be
nonverbal and immediately understood.

It is helpful to plan the general strategy of the match beforehand. There should also be advance agreement on who will
take the overhead in the middle of the court, and on whose
backhand or forehand is stronger (for those shots which do
not clearly belong to one player or the other).

It is advisable that one of the players informally act as a
team captain. Margaret Court suggests that, in mixed doubles, it works best if the woman lets the man be the captain.
Nevertheless, she is firm in saying that the woman should not
be the junior partner. Other professionals would agree.

Know Your Partner

Partners must know each other's physical capabilities, and
they must know each other's tactical idiosyncrasies. Jaime

Fillol feels that doubles partners should know each other so well that each knows not just what the other *can* do but what he *will* do. The Amritraj brothers have played as a team for so long that they have the moves of a military drill company. Their precision is as good as though it were rehearsed. They move up and back together, usually one slightly forward of the other, so as to be ready for a crossover. They use the I or tandem formation, they cross simultaneously, and they cover for each other as if computerized.

To "know thy partner" requires more intensive concentration than in singles. While all the elements of concentration are still vital, there must be an additional awareness of the position of one's partner. This secondary concentration is analogous to peripheral vision. In soccer, Pelé's adjunctive concentration is masterful. His peripheral vision is superior; and, while dribbling the ball at a fast run, he is acutely aware of where his teammates and the opposition are. Doubles players must develop this kind of adjunctive or peripheral concentration, but it must supplement rather than take precedence over the primary focus of attention—the ball.

Mixed Doubles

The psychological factors valid for doubles hold for mixed doubles as well. One modifying factor is that the attitudes of the male partner may more easily influence the play of the female than vice versa.

To be good at mixed doubles, a man must be simpatico toward women while, at the same time, evoking an aggressive style of play. If he shows by his actions and facial expressions that he considers it a great misfortune to be stuck with such an inept partner, it may raise her arousal level; but psyching up one's partner is not without danger. An approach which reassures and encourages is more certain of success.

The self-respect and self-confidence of a woman playing mixed doubles tends to derive little nourishment from direct, individual criticism, constructive or not. The magic words are: "C'mon, *we* can do it," and "Right on, partner."

There are few other sports where a husband and wife can team together. But there are problems with husband-wife pairings. Spouses tend to be less inhibited toward each other than are unrelated partners. A husband will more easily criticize his own wife than someone else's. A wife who shows disappointment in her husband's poor play will probably suppress her feelings with another partner. In addition, the player making the poor shot will more easily become irritated at his or her spouse for reacting critically.

Not only is conflict likely, but there may also be rivalry between the husband and wife. In the 1960s, Carole Graebner was a finalist in singles at Forest Hills and her husband, Clark, was on the Davis Cup team. Carole, with a higher ranking than Clark, was the breadwinner. When they teamed in doubles, Clark informed her that "there can be only one captain of the team, and you're not it." The competition between them, intensified by the media, became so difficult that they decided to find different mixed-doubles partners.

Each tennis-playing married couple must make the decision as to what is best for them. If winning is rather important, they probably are best off with other partners. They are more likely to get along as partners if their motive for playing tennis is recreational.

CHAPTER NINE

Losers

IN tennis, as in life, the easiest thing to be is a loser—to give in, drop out, go under.

A player may be both physically fit and sufficiently skilled in all the basic moves. He may be situationally creative. Yet, against an opponent of roughly comparable skill, he may still lose—and not because his game is fundamentally unsound. Rather, the player is, in effect, compelled to lose by forces almost totally extraneous to the game of tennis.

And, in tennis, as in life, it is all too possible to win and still be a loser—to be a thief of victory.

Losers fall into roughly three categories. Character-dictated losers, including gamesmen and "funny" feeders, are compelled to win by practically any means. They are so highly motivated to win that they will sacrifice principle to expediency. In tennis, such individuals elevate what is ostensibly a game—a form of diversion—to the status of a life-and-death struggle. They have much to prove and much to lose. Some character-dictated losers actually regard winning as a kind of death. Compelled to lose in order to remain safe from harm, they have been psyched-out by the past. They have much to prove, and most of it is puerile.

The second large group consists of situation-dictated losers. These individuals—some of them winning players in hundreds of other games—are psyched-out by their own perceptions of a specific opponent or type of opponent. They are more highly motivated to retain their misperceptions than they are to win.

While the character- and situation-dictated losers are actually playing tennis, some psychosocially-dictated losers are hard at work at a wholly different game. Having been molded to be losers, they aid and abet this abyssmal situation by lacking the motivation to escape it. For some of these individuals, tennis is simply a tool. For others, it serves as a mask, a bit of camouflage to cover or distort the fact that they are not really alive.

The Gamesman

Since psychological ploys have been used for centuries, it is probable that the entire concept of gamesmanship is rooted in antiquity. Mothers must have been laying guilt on their children since before the advent of recorded history, and the confidence game must be equally ancient. Thus, we need neither Machiavelli nor Eric Berne to tell us about the psychological games played in many phases of interpersonal relationships. Everyday observation reveals the unabashed frankness with which both the work and recreational activity of many individuals is focused upon making "points."

The Gambits

When Stephan Potter formalized and set down in writing his principles of gamesmanship, he gave examples of their use in many sports, including tennis. In fact, he credits a particular tennis match with the crystallization of the concept. Potter elaborates various gambits, the primary goals of which are: (1) to instill guilt in your opponent; (2) to demean his upbringing, generosity, knowledge, or values, (3) to convince him that you are inexplicably lucky and that the fates are against him; (4) to make him feel like a novice; and (5) to control the pace of the game.

According to Potter, subtlety and variation are the mark of the sophisticated practitioner. The basic requirements are that the technique be imaginative and elegant. The gambits are to be executed with such finesse that one's opponent is unaware that there is any ulterior purpose to them whatsoever. Applying these ideas to tennis, Potter notes that when his opponent was about to serve, he (Potter) might scold a noisy spectator. The purpose of the scolding—breaking the opponent's rhythm—would be accomplished, and with class. Ostensibly, Potter was not scolding on his own account, but because it was ill-mannered of the spectator to shout just as Potter's worthy opponent was about to serve.

Potter also tells of a 65-year-old chap who said he was "never beaten in a key match by any decently brought-up boy under twenty-five." He seemed to accomplish the feat by initiating a train of thought in the mind of the younger player to the effect that it would be unsporting to beat anyone as old as he by too wide a margin. It then became an easy matter to allow the younger player to expect him to tire in the last couple of sets. Then, perhaps augmented by whatever degree of Oedipal conflict the young man might possess, the guilt stakes would imperceptibly be raised to winning and losing the entire match.

When Potter first came out with his classic theory, gamesmanship must have been, if not a total spoof, at least 85 percent spoof. The trouble is that its gambits were applied seriously by both Americans and Englishmen; and gamesmanship came to stay. Its forms in tennis are many, mean, varied, usually clumsy, and often crass. They range from the condescending "Good try, it was only out by an inch"; through the guilt-evoking "I hope I will give you a good enough game, since my back is still a little stiff from that runaway horse I caught last week"; to merely delaying the game in order to change rackets or headbands. One gamesman we encountered told occasional jokes during the match. In addition to breaking concentration, laughter effectively inhibits any strength of contraction of the voluntary muscles.

Countering Gamesmanship

If your opponent employs gamesmanship tactics, you have three choices, other than walking off the court or threatening him with bodily injury. You can (1) be cool and detached, and ignore him, (2) ridicule his actions by mimicking him, or (3) if he stalls or if he distracts you just before a shot, make the shot anyway, and smash it as hard as you can. If it goes in, take the point. If it goes out, declare a let ball in accordance with the rules and regulations. If he gets his dander up, explain that the rules state that if an opponent unintentionally distracts or disconcerts a player, a let ball shall be called; if the act is deliberate, a point shall be awarded to the other player. Tell him that you would not imagine that he would intentionally try to upset your concentration; and so, you will just play the point over, thank you. We would advise this third choice only in instances of unmitigated gamesmanship. Otherwise, you will be known as "the nut with the rule book." Alternatively, you might apply a bit of gentle gamesmanship of your own—if you must.

Compared to the sophisticated gambits delineated by Potter, most of Ilie Nastase's efforts at gamesmanship are crass. His opponents sometimes feel called upon to counter them. In a 1974 W.C.T. match, for example, Jan Kodes walked over to the sidelines and sat down to wait for Nastase to complete his act. In 1975, Arthur Ashe was less patient. After more than two minutes of cooling his heels while Nastase lectured a number of spectators on manners and civility, Ashe announced, "I claim a default," and walked off the court. It is surprising that no one else has ever used Clark Graebner's inventive counterstrategy of several years earlier. Reacting to the fact that Nastase was both delaying the game and vocally harassing him, Graebner leaped over the net and went for him with an upraised racket. The blow was never struck, but the threat was enough to put Nastase on his best behavior for the rest of the match.

The "Success"

Strivings for achievement are sometimes confused with strivings for success, and the person possessed by strong desires for success is often willing to help the confusion along.

A mimic and a thief of form, rather than a worker at content, many of this individual's traits are opposite to those of the high achiever. His motivation is extrinsic, and he exhibits a proportionately higher level of anxiety. Instead of working to develop the skills necessary for achievement, he tries to emulate the achiever. Wanting desperately to be considered an achiever, he attempts to get there by way of ploy and appearance.

As a general rule, the tennis player strongly motivated to succeed will resort to gamesmanship. He will give himself the benefit of the doubt on close calls, talk a good game off court, and tend to dress more like a tennis player than an actual tennis player ever does.

Although he will never be a good player, his "success"-oriented behavior is quite valuable for making contacts. Compared to the courts, however, the golf course, the clubhouse bar, and the steamroom are equally or even more fertile fields for his pursuits.

"Funny Feeders": Seekers After the Ultimate Performance

Except under extraordinary conditions, a certain percentage of an individual's maximum performance capacity remains inaccessible. This reserve is a protective mechanism, ensuring that neither physiological and metabolic exhaustion nor injury to muscles, tendons, and ligaments occurs. This reserve is variously estimated at between 20 and 50 percent.

Many athletes will go to any length to improve performance. Too many feel that improvement will come from unlocking this autonomously protected reserve. In their constant search for the key, athletes have employed meditative techniques, hypnosis, drugs, dietary supplements, and exotic diets. While the first two may be useful in improving some players' concentration, the others are at best risky and at worst fatal.

Drug Takers

In the use of drugs, the idiosyncrasies of the individual brain can be as crucial as dosage level. A single neuroactive drug can cause different, sometimes opposite, reactions in different people. One man who recognized this phenomenon was Sigmund Freud. Noting that the effects of cocaine on himself were different from its effects on others, he accurately surmised that individual disposition played a major role in type and level of reaction.

There are other examples. Most users are sedated by barbiturates; but a paradoxical effect occurs in patients with porphyria, a metabolic defect in which they become hyperactive when given this class of drugs. Even the grassroots pharmacologists of the drug culture have noted that some of their novitiates experience "bad trips," while others get "high" from the same batch of stuff.

Drugs may improve athletic performance, but improvement has its costs. For example, adrenalin (epinephrine) makes the heart beat faster with greater force, and dilates the bronchioles. But endurance suffers. Thus, the cost of greater cardiac output is lessened cardiac efficiency, and proportionately greater oxygen consumption by the heart muscle. Under the influence of another familiar drug, amphetamine, fatigue (the usual vehicle of the protected reserve) is inhibited and mental alertness is increased. But the cost here is decreased concentration. Amphetamine use in sports presents a special danger: when fatigue and physiological exhaustion coincide, the athlete runs a grave health risk. Following amphetamine use, cyclists and distance runners have been known to collapse during competition. At least two have died.

Diet Skewers

The complexity of human biochemistry is sufficient reason to assume that there are no dietary panaceas. Neither avacados nor rice, nor any one vitamin, nor quick-energy candy bars, nor bananas, nor chicken soup will ensure optimim function. Variety alone holds the key.

Much of one's psychological well-being depends upon the amount of the amino acid tryptophan that reaches the brain. Synthesis of the biogenic amine serotonin, depends to a great extent upon it. And when serotonin synthesis decreases, bleak days increase. Since food is the ultimate source of tryptophan, there have been some recent advocates of increased intake of foods rich in tryptophan. Unfortunately for them, the philosophy that "If one of something is good for you, two must be twice as good" does not hold true in this case.

Danger dwells in diets rich in *selected* amino acids. Too much of one can inhibit the production and utilization of others. The biochemistry of the brain is a complex of possibilities, probabilities, influences, and feedback. Brain chemistry is in a constant state of flux, and the equilibrium which exists is a precarious one.

Tryptophan is not the only "magic" cure-all. In the commonly held belief that if a muscle gets a quick shot of glucose, it will have extra energy for contraction, some athletes become candy bar freaks. But things are not quite so simple with the human organism. In order for a candy bar to provide the glucose which will, in turn, provide the energy for muscle contraction, it has to be eaten anywhere from two hours to two days before the time the muscle actually contracts. Ingestion of candy bars boosts sugar prices more than muscular efficiency.

On the other hand, the candy bar can have a psychological benefit. During moderate exercise, such as tennis, blood glucose decreases. Since adequate levels of blood glucose operate in maintaining a positive outlook, that candy bar eaten just before play begins has this bit of redeeming value: while it will not help the player move faster or hit harder, sometime toward the middle of the match it may help to cheer him up a bit.

The immediate, last-step energy source for muscle contraction is provided by the high-energy chemical bonds of adenosine triphosphate (ATP), which is normally found in high concentration in muscle tissue. Once a molecule of ATP gives up the energy from one of its chemical bonds, it must be resynthesized by the body. If this did not occur, the ATP would be used up at three games to love, and the player could not last out a set.

Although ATP can be resynthesized in several ways, the

principal energy pool for its maintenance is phosphocreatine (PC), a molecule with energy-rich phosphate bonds. Increases in work load decrease PC levels in muscle.

At maximal work loads, PC levels will drop to zero, and ATP levels will be at 60 percent of their previous values. At this point, no further muscle work can be done. The tennis player who reaches zero PC levels might not have enough energy left to call for an emergency gin and tonic.

The body has an additional, large reserve of energy in muscle glycogen—molecules of glucose linked together. This is the major, ultimate energy source for muscle contraction. In mild to moderate exercise (such as tennis), glycogen, free fatty acids, and/or blood glucose are together utilized by the muscle tissue to keep PC and ATP levels high. Here glucose can substitute for free fatty acids. As exercise becomes more strenuous, the percentage of energy derived from glycogen increases until, at maximal effort, it is supplying almost the entire amount. But the muscle glycogen must be there beforehand, since its resynthesis does not begin until more than two hours after heavy exercise.

Diet exerts a strong influence on resynthesis of muscle glycogen. A diet rich in carbohydrates will restore depleted supplies of muscle glycogen within twenty-four hours. Moreover, the glycogen levels will continue to rise for another two days, providing a greater energy reserve than normal. This is called the overshoot effect. Weight lifters, cross-country skiers, and athletes in a few other sports have intuitively recognized the glycogen overshoot effect. Weight men, for instance, will train until total fatigue two days before competition, and then do little more than limber up and feast on sweets until the meet.

Recently, some athletes have pressed muscle glycogen loading to its limits, and initial competitive performances have been exceptional. But the latest research indicates that short-term advantage is being traded off against long-term cost:

muscle glycogen overloading is responsible for some degree of muscle fiber destruction.

Certain impatient, foolish, and credulous people, having heard that potassium has a way of doing something which will let a player run faster and hit a tennis ball harder, attempt to absorb large amounts of potassium in order to improve their performance. In fact, the potassium ion is associated with increased muscle blood flow; increased potassium levels do result in greater vascular relaxation and, consequently, a bigger, faster supply of blood and more muscle work. But an imbalance in potassium levels is dangerous, for potassium is multifunctional. It is involved not only in muscle contraction but also in impulse transmission in nerves. Moreover, potassium is a significant factor in the acid-base balance of human metabolism. Low potassium may cause muscle weakness; high potassium is lethal.

In terms of diet, it probably will not do much good to stuff oneself with such well-known potassium-rich foods as oranges, bananas, and chicken soup. Providing one's kidney function is good, increased potassium intake probably cannot raise the blood levels of potassium enough to significantly affect the mechanics of striated muscle vasodilation. The body's homeostatic mechanisms will often defeat the self-destructiveness of this brand of "funny feeder."

Hoping to bring about an increase in their speed and reaction time, some players seek a dietary increase in blood calcium level. Like potassium, calcium is heavily involved in muscle contraction and metabolism. Without adequate calcium, the electrical changes (depolarization) preceding muscle contraction cannot take place. Potassium may be ready to leave the cell, but it will not do so unless calcium is there to replace it.

Here again, the "funny feeders" are misguided. Although the source of calcium is the diet, the body's blood calcium levels are only slightly influenced by an increase in the amount of calcium in the diet. Hormones (particularly parathyroid) and dietary intake of wheat, protein, and vitamin D exert much stronger influences. Attempts to raise blood calcium levels by means of focused diet will usually prove ineffective because, if these become too high, excess calcium will be excreted rather than absorbed through the intestines. Furthermore, if calcium levels *are* raised too high, there is a risk of imbalance between the body's calcium and phosphorus levels. Such an imbalance can impede the resynthesis of ATP.

Again, the true wisdom is in variety and moderation. The autonomously protected reserve and the body's homeostatic mechanisms are not a foolproof safeguard against the ego needs of both the competitive player who will go to any lengths to win and the individual who considers the body as little more than the abject servant of the mind.

The "In" Player

Over the past few years, tennis has become an "in" activity. In some suburban areas and smaller towns, tennis has become a way of separating the eternal sheep from the current goats. During the outdoor tennis season particularly, some who do not play are observed to feel "left out," and to grow markedly cooler toward those members of their social group who do play and who essentially have formed an even more "in" subgroup.

Signaling which group they "really" belong to, suburban housewives can be observed doing their supermarket shopping in tennis outfits, regardless of whether they are actual players. Others are seen taking lessons with some regularity, but are never seen actually playing. A few individuals, most of them women, are never seen either taking lessons or playing, but may be observed with some regularity clustered about the sidelines, dressed in the most fashionable outfits—color coordinated and spotlessly fresh.

There is a period in practically everyone's life when it is of extreme psychic importance to be like a select few of the others. This is also the time of great expectations, of a sometimes tenuous, sometimes wondrously overpowering belief that one is truly meant for all things good and beautiful and true. This is when one must believe, if one is to endure the psychic pain intrinsic to the period, that one is not like the horde of others, but instead clearly superior—if not outwardly, then inwardly—and possessed of a wonderful something which the vast majority of people (clods, fools, and old folks that they are) simply cannot see. This period is adolescence, and many individuals never outgrow it.

While this type of stunted growth does keep divorce lawyers, psychiatrists, singles bars, and the encounter, fashion, and cosmetics industries very busy, it does not result in either satisfying lives or good tennis. Moving from one activity or fad to another, joining and abandoning one social group after another, hoping against hope for any form of salvation which will elevate them to actuality, many of these perpetual adolescents continue their search. They live for tomorrow, count on tomorrow's luck; and their search cannot help but end in disillusion, depression, and defeat. Too late, when all but a few of their tomorrows are gone, age forces "in" players to realize that their time has been misused, their potential has vanished, and their skills have remained undeveloped.

The magically perfect group doing perfect things in perfect ways is never to be found. It never existed. And although some games fit some personalities better than others, the perfect game does not exist. Ask any highly skilled tennis player what he really thinks of the game. It can only be, at its best, a fantastic challenge. Like any other activity at its best, the game is process; it holds no ultimate answers.

Faddists tend to remain faddists; winning players go on to become better winning players; and while the twain may meet on the courts, their personalities will always be different. The difference is evident in the winning player's recognition that imitation, faddism, and luck do not bring perfection in anything to anyone. Driven and egocentric though he or she may be, the winning player recognizes that no one is perfect; that practically nothing can simultaneously be good, beautiful, and true; that all anyone can count on are the grief and goodness of today; and that it is through work that one approximates perfection.

The Submissives

There are many tennis players who are regularly defeated by certain other players, even though the actual abilities involved are almost equal. A dominant-submissive relationship exists between such winners and losers. Much of what constitutes their relationship has its basis less in reality than in the pair's mutual perception of reality. Because of the needs and desires of both individuals, the self-perception of each is mirrored and reinforced by the perception of the other.

Three factors are involved: aggressiveness, self-confidence, and "strength of personality." The first two combine what is actually there with each person's need-dominated perception of what should be there. After all, it is next to impossible to be thought of as aggressive and self-confident if one does not actually look, act, and to some degree feel that way. In contrast, a "strong" personality dwells almost entirely in the per-

ception of the beholder. Such "strength" is an attributed quality which inheres more in the projected needs, desires, and
values of the loser than in characteristics actually possessed by
the "strong" winner.

Strength of character involves a kind of aura of superiority
attained and perpetuated only in small part by overt, "confident" aggressiveness. It cannot be gained through tantrum,
brutality, or gamesmanship. Myth is very helpful to the establishment of the quality, and the loser's desire to believe in
"magic" is usually of considerable aid in its perpetuation.

Here is an example. Ross Case's fellow Australians say that
he is the living embodiment of good luck. Before a match,
other players will concede the choice of serving first: "Forget
the spin, Ross will win it anyway." They nicknamed him
"Snake" as tribute to his luck. (In Australia, where the mon-
goose never made it and kangaroos are vegetarians, snakes are
considered lucky.) In the final round of the Alan King–
Caesar's Palace tournament, Case came within a tie-breaker
of winning. Despite his loss, the promoters decided that the
match was so close and so exciting that they would award
both finalists the same top prize money; and Case walked
off with an extra $15,000 for a tennis "first." The myth of his
"luck" was enhanced, and with it his psychological dominance over his opponents.

A common type of dominance-submission in tennis involves the psychophysical intimidation of one player by
another. Among the touring professionals, Margaret Court
provides striking evidence. Rangy and rawboned, she moves to
the net quickly, where the long, strong arm and the "weapon"
it holds are physically intimidating. Although Billie Jean
King has neither equivalent physical stature nor comparable
strength, she does have the best volley in the game, and can
put away the ball with such authority that she is equally dis-
quieting to an opponent. These two women long dominated
women's tennis.

On the men's side, the classic example is Pancho Gonzales, who decimated the opposition in the 1950s. Jack Kramer described playing against him as "holding a tiger at bay." Gonzales had the physical attributes of raw power, spark-gap reflexes, and speed. His service and overhead were awesome. Gonzales remembers that when Jack Kramer beat him on tour in 1949, he decided that the Durocher maxim "Nice guys finish last" held some truth, and he thereupon changed from good to good-and-mean.

It is probable that what Gonzales did when he rose from defeat in the form of a tiger was to apply some psychology: he set about to behave "as if," and thereby to trick the perception of his opponents. Only nice guys who have been bitten by werewolves can actually change that dramatically—and they usually do it only when the moon is full. Gonzales must have acted in such a way as to make his opponents think of him as ferocious and mean; consciously or unconsciously he became, in their perception, a beast of awesome raw power. In short, he psyched them out—heightened their anxiety and diverted their concentration—before they had even begun to play.

For varying lengths of time, a suggestible individual can actually perceive as reality the "as if" role he or she plays. Good actors do it until the final curtain. Therefore, it is possible that Gonzales succeeded in psyching himself up to the point where he, too, believed that he had switched from good to good-and-mean as swiftly and easily as his opponents came to believe he had.

Another example of such suggestibility is the story about Gussie Moran at the zoo. In 1949 she reportedly spent an afternoon at the Central Park Zoo in order to "absorb courage from the lions." After that, she is described as having been like a great cat on the court—she not only won the match but the tournament as well.

Billie Jean King exhibits classical dominance. In part because of it, she has singlehandedly done more to eliminate sex discrimination in sports than anyone had imagined possible. And because she has done what she has done, Billie Jean is more than a heroine to the younger players; she is a living legend. This heroine worship in turn gives her a psychological hold over the younger players. Her dominance also has been, and still is, felt by women who are her contemporaries.

For instance, Rosemary Casals has a shameful record against Billie Jean. It may be that Billie Jean is the better player, but no one would hold the difference to be in proportion to their won-lost record. Carole Graebner recalls her amateur days when she and Billie Jean were close friends on the tournament circuit: "When we played singles, Billie Jean always won. Later, when I was away from her, I could beat her." Virginia Wade, too, feels Billie Jean's strength of personality on the court. Just after winning in the W.T.T. singles against her, Virginia said that Billie Jean was technically vulnerable but almost unbeatable mentally.

Perceived dominance, or the ability to seem "almost unbeatable mentally," is by no means the sole province of women. In 1968, Arthur Ashe was an amateur and, at least in financial terms, Rod Laver was a pro. The two met in the semifinals of the first open Wimbledon tournament. Laver won, and since then he has owned Ashe. Bob Lutz could rarely beat his doubles partner, Stan Smith. Jimmy Connors has a tournament record of winning against just about everyone, and he is contemptuous of most of his opponents. The exception is Ilie Nastase, his doubles partner, against whom he has a losing record.

Personal closeness between two players may result in a dominant-submissive relationship. Not everyone finds it easy to be aggressive toward a sister, a roommate, a friend, or a doubles partner. Jean and Chris Evert, two sisters, provide an example. Long-term doubles teams like Rosemary Casals and Billie Jean King offer another. A submissive-dominant pattern did not arise in the doubles team of Ann Haydon Jones and Virginia Wade. But when they had to face each other in singles, each felt the pressures and conflicts so intensely and equally that for no other reason they decided to break up the team.

Actual personal closeness need not be the factor making for reluctance to play the aggressive game necessary to win. Implicit closeness—as why the opponent is perceived as possessing characteristics similar to those of an individual important in the loser's life—can be equally powerful. Implied and/or actual characteristics of that important individual are substituted for the actual traits of the opponent. The loser behaves submissively, responding as if the opponent were in fact that individual, and forfeits the game before play even begins. Infantile fears of retribution are apparently involved here. The important person represents a parent, and the loser's unconscious equates winning with the murder of that parent. Thus, the submissive player restrains his play in fear of the imagined consequences of aggression. Others—less submissive—may, in the framework of rebellion, find in tennis the symbolic means to wish fulfillment.

Julia and Julian and Carl and Jack: A Case Study

Those who are psyched-out by the past are pawns of the present. They are moved by the situation; they do not dominate it.

Too often tennis players are less tennis players than sons and lovers, mothers and fathers, gods and relics from other places and other times. A player may have different roles with different opponents. Thus, there are tennis triangles, quadrilaterals, and polygons.

Julia and Julian

Julia is a far better player than most women. A strong amateur, she usually plays against men, since most women cannot give her the fast, aggressive game which a man routinely can. Julia and Julian are closely matched in tennis ability.

Julian is a steady baseline player, strong and accurate, but not aggressive. He is socially shy. Gentlemanly, even gallant, he invariably treated Julia with considerable respect. When playing against her, he would always retrieve any netted balls on either side, and would give her the benefit of the doubt on close calls. When she was at the net, he would never smash the ball right at her. He enjoyed long rallies and would only occasionally hit for outright winners. Julian played his best within these psychological boundaries. Although on a conscious level he tried to win and never gave away any points, Julian never succeeded in winning against Julia.

Off court, Julian was as courteous toward Julia as he was on court. There was never the slightest physical contact between them, not even a touch on the arm.

Julia and Carl

Carl is not shy. Off court, he never hesitated to place a hand on Julia's shoulder or give her a friendly hug. On court, however, all of Carl's affection was transformed into aggressive play; and winning became all-consuming. When Julia was at the net, she was under constant threat of being hit. When Julia was ahead in score, Carl would pout and stamp like a petulant child. Julia would have liked to beat Carl, but she never did.

Once, Carl told Julia a detailed story of a time when, as a

child, he beat his father at chess. Julia's reply was, "Don't you realize your father let you win?"

Julia and Jack

Julia's attitude toward Jack is quite different from her attitude toward either Julian or Carl. Her game against Jack was also different. Although she played him regularly, and they too are closely matched in tennis ability, she was never able to beat him.

Julia never felt that she could play her usual aggressive game against someone who so commanded her respect. Jack is a doctor.

Julian and Carl

Julian and Carl played only occasionally, and almost invariably Julian won. Here his steadiness made the difference.

Their matches were often punctuated by personal friction over line calls, tennis etiquette, and the like. In one match, after a bit of minor discord, Julian hit a searing cross-court drive which bounced close to the baseline and which Carl could not reach. Julian thought it a clean winner. Carl thought it clearly out and did not hesitate to call it the way he saw or wished to see it.

Deciding that too much was enough, Julian walked off the court and never played Carl again.

Analysis

Here we have what appears to be one woman and three men playing four games of tennis; but what we have, operationally, is three women and four men playing what only appears to be four games of tennis. In each of these games, at least one person is not really playing tennis against another tennis player but, instead, is playing some entirely different game against a totally different opponent.

Even though Julia has transcended the customary role of the female tennis player—she is aggressive, does not duck, and plays hard and fast—she has yet to progress to the point where she is simply playing tennis. On court, she usually alternates between two of the three roles which adult females are expected to play, and customarily do play, in one-to-one relationships with adult males: "Little Girl" and "Big Mama." But against one opponent she regresses even further.

Julia nurtures Julian and, at those times when he turns sulky, Carl. Here she is Big Mama. When Carl is merely aggressive, she plays Little Girl to his game of "Nasty Kid." In her games against Jack, however, she regresses to childhood, playing a game triggered by childish attitudes having to do with "I love you, doctor, because doctors are good and nice and everything, and they take care of little things like me." Which, of course, Jack does: he beats her, every time.

Julian plays two roles: "Nice Kid" and "Well-Bred Parent." Against Julia, Julian's game is more than choked, it is crippled. The attitude dominating Julian's playing has to do with "I am a well-trained boy. I know that mothers, sisters, aunts, grandmas, and teachers will love me only if I am *very* good." Being overtly aggressive toward females, even when it involved winning fair and square, was obviously not included in Julian's socialization. To the detriment of the majority of Julian's mixed-singles games, his socialization was no doubt carried out by a domineering, demanding, rejecting, sexist woman. In his games against Carl, Julian plays as an adult, but like many adults he must have known, he is too irritated by the antics of an unruly child. Here, Julian plays the Well-Bred Parent.

Carl exhibits greater role consistency than do either Julia or Julian. He plays Nasty Kid with everyone.

It is probable that off court, Julia is even "nicer," more compliant. If she brings such roles into a game, it follows that they must dominate her off-court life to an even greater extent. She has designated tennis as an outlet for some portion of negative aggression, but she remains too tied to the past to make good use of it.

Julia is probably right—Carl's father did let him win that chess game. Carl seems to have been manipulating nice, parenting adults into letting him win quite a lot of games, for quite a long time.

Psychology should not be used as an excuse for failure. Versions of "I can't win now because Mother wouldn't let me then" make poor crutches. That game is over. Psychological and psychoanalytic concepts are tools for self-understanding and self-actualization. To use them as excuses for poor performance will only hinder the player.

It is probable that, for most recreational players, attempts at desensitization by repeatedly playing a dominant opponent will be to no avail. Too little learning and too many defeats, both psychic and actual, will occur before the all-important win. Rather, on a game-by-game basis, the player's focus of concentration should be narrowed from the opponent and the consequences of winning to the move of the moment. Play by play and point by point, the player must work the moves in isolation, with no thought of before or after.

Of course, there are other possibilities. You can imitate a winning player you know, or, like Gussie Moran, you can go to the zoo. But the choice is that of "feel" and not of "think." You must psych yourself into the role, slide down into it during warmup, and stay there. If during the course of the game you begin to tighten up, you must not switch roles but must focus further in. If specific aspects of the past continue to exert so powerful an influence as to break concentration and actively divert attention from the real purpose of play, then for the sake of both self and game, the most productive solution may be counseling.

The Self-Defeated

There are other players who rarely win. Throughout their lives they follow patterns of self-defeat. In fact, it is psychologically imperative that they not win.

The psyches of many of us contain at least some small element of self-defeat, but often it goes unrecognized. However, plenty of it finds its way onto the tennis court. And it can pervade any and all facets of one's life. Wherever achievement and self-actualization should ordinarily be expected, insidious self-defeat may be found at work.

Samuel J. Warner has shown that the reasons for self-defeat are several and often hidden from obvious view. Anxiety, guilt, hostility, and the need for acceptance are but a few of the reasons; and, paradoxically, even the will to power can operate as the force leading to the will to self-defeat.

One of the ways in which self-defeat manifests itself is through the goals which the individual sets. These goals are direct results of the type and degree of aggression which he allows himself to express. The competitive nature of tennis offers an excellent vehicle for the ritualization and rationalization of defeat for those who cannot focus the aggression necessary for self-actualization. If his goals are too low, the player will never progress and will always be anxious as to his effectiveness in more challenging situations. If he sets his goals so high that failure is certain, he either will remain at a standstill or will regress.

Those who are motivated by self-defeat tend to choose

goals which are extreme in their degree of difficulty. The chosen goal is either so easily achieved that success is virtually guaranteed, or so difficult that it will provide an intrinsic excuse for failure. There are players who never really play but are forever taking lessons from instructors who build egos. These players never lose, but neither do they ever grow. At the other extreme are those players who always play opponents a class above them, thereby almost surely guaranteeing their own defeat.

Self-defeat may come by way of "letdown." It is not uncommon for a player to win three or four games in a row, only to have his opponent "catch fire," taking the next three or four games and perhaps the set. Pancho Gonzales advises that playing every point intensely is the counteraction to the "letdown" phenomenon.

The force of self-defeat can be subversive at any level. A pro battles his way to the very top. Then, at that very last moment, his self-defeatist psyche goes into action, telling him, "Now, there will be no celebration in winning. Winning is expected of you. All you can do, now, is keep from losing." Or self-defeat may operate through fear. World-class and weekend players alike are afflicted by the fear of losing, particularly to an inferior player. What we fear will happen, we tend to *expect* will happen. Then the defeatist self-fulfilling prophecy takes over: the psyche sees to it that what is expected to happen does, in fact, occur.

A frequently successful solution to this "expectation" dilemma is to assume a pose of self-confidence. Although ostensibly for the benefit of the opponent, this assumed attitude will tend to slyly creep into your own outlook. (Since too much of a good thing can be detrimental, you should, of course, strive to strike a balance between the extremes of fear and overconfidence.) Then the psyche once again sets expectation and the self-fulfilling prophecy in action—only this time, hopefully, to the benefit of the player.

Losers

We have reviewed the many avenues leading to losing. They exert a negative influence on ego and personality. They are dead ends on the journey to self-realization.

All individuals cannot be winners all of the time, especially in tennis. They can, however, have their fair share of winning and feel a satisfaction in a strong and true attempt at it.

Tennis, not having life-serious implications, may be a good first step for the loser to enter into the ways of reality. The next steps in real life may then be a little easier.

CHAPTER TEN

Women vs. Men

IN the psychological realm of losing, women and men are equally vulnerable. Psyching oneself out plays no sexual favorites.

Yet performance records indicate that in almost every sport the best men can beat the best women—not just most of the time, but every time. In tennis, Margaret Court is the first to admit that she could not touch the top forty male tennis players. Chris Evert, who cuts through singles opponents like a chain saw through saplings, agrees but lowers the number to thirty. If a list actually were to be made, the number of men who could consistently beat the top women would likely run to over 100—which shows where Bobby Riggs ranks in the scheme of things.

In general, men run and throw in a more athletic fashion than women do. Their reflexes are faster, their movements are more rapidly coordinated, their muscles contract more explosively. Women are more supple and their joints are more flexible. Their movements seem more rhythmic; they appear to move more gracefully. Are these characteristics innate—determined by genetic, physical, and chemical factors? Or are they determined by societal roles set for each sex?

Women vs. Men

Physiological Factors

On average, the differences in lower-body bone structure give men only a slight edge in those sports, such as tennis, which involve running. The major bone of the leg, the femur, is not straight with a nob on each end, as a cartoonist might portray it. Rather, it is angled near the upper end, next to the hip joint. In females, the angle between the neck and the shaft of the femur is comparatively more acute, and the hip joint is set facing to the side and slightly forward. They are so positioned to accommodate the width, depth, and tilt of a pelvis capable of childbearing. In males, the hip joint faces directly sideways, and even if the difference in total skeletal size is taken into account, the head (or ball) of the femur is significantly larger.

As we walk or run, each foot does not strike the ground in a vertical line beneath its corresponding hip joint. Rather, the bones of the leg form an angle with that vertical line, so that the feet will be close to the midline. The greater the angle of the femur from the vertical, the less efficient is one's running.

Overall, however, the male-female difference in femur angulation is not great. Bone to bone measurements reveal men with relatively wide hips and women with relatively narrow ones; and some orthopedic surgeons use the same hip pin angulation for both men and women.

One area of difference is reach. The shoulder girdle is smaller in women than in men of equivalent height. Women's hands are also proportionately smaller. The average 70″ male has a 7.5″ hand, while the average 64″ female has a 6.5″ hand. The implications for tennis are obvious. In this area, men generally surpass women.

While males usually surpass females in absolute strength, males are closely matched with females in measured strength. That is, if strength of the lower body is considered relative to weight (or, better, to lean-body weight), male-female ratios are comparable. Under the microscope, male and female muscle tissues look much the same, but males' muscle contractions are more explosive. And while males can move to the net faster and hit every type of stroke harder, females are generally more supple. The lesser flexibility of men is primarily determined not by the muscles and tendons, which provide for movement of the bones or for holding them in a fixed position, but by the ligaments which form the joints between the bones.

The greater flexibility of women is evident in figure skating and in gymnastics. Men would not stand a chance on the balance beam against the likes of Olga Korbut or Nadia Comaneci. They wisely avoid that event and stick to such apparatus as the rings, pommel horse, and high bar, which require a generous portion of strength above the waist.

Interesting as these comparisons are, they do not answer the basic question: Why are women's records poorer than men's in sports like tennis, where great absolute strength is not required—where, indeed, it is of secondary advantage?

Psychophysiological Factors

The key psychophysiological issues are hormones and reaction time.

Hormones

Hormonal influences seem to favor male muscle in absolute strength and in explosiveness. Metabolism and psychophysiological responses to stress are influenced by the endocrine glands, among which are the producers of testosterone and estrogen. Although males and females have both hormones, male levels of testosterone are far greater, as are female levels of estrogen.

Testosterone levels influence muscle mass and development. A male who is trained with close to maximal work loads for given muscles will gain both in strength and enlargement of those muscles, while a similarly trained female will gain more in strength than in muscle size.

The strength and enlargement (hypertrophy) of muscle mass depends in part on circulating testosterone levels. Testosterone is the major metabolic tissue-building (anabolic) hormone, although estrogen, too, has some anabolic function. Testosterone stimulates muscle fiber growth. It is commonly recognized that exercise in the presence of high testosterone levels will produce greater muscle hypertrophy. Specific muscles, such as the biceps and deltoid, seem more susceptible than others.

R. D. Adams, a Harvard authority in neurophysiology, states that postpuberty male muscle fiber exceeds equivalent female muscle fiber in strength and endurance, as well as in volume. However, Jack H. Wilmore, the respected California physiologist, does not agree, believing that women can increase their strength markedly, even without a corresponding increase in muscle size. The implication is that, with adequate training, nonhypertrophic female muscle can match hypertrophic male muscle in all but such extreme sports as weight lifting, football, and boxing.

It is possible that testosterone also affects the transmission of nerve impulses. Research indicates that testosterone can influence at least the development of some central nervous system synapses in animals.

Testosterone exerts an influence on the behavior of both animals and man. Mental depression is not uncommon in men of middle age, when testosterone levels decrease sharply. Castration, and the resultant sharp reduction in testosterone levels, renders tomcats more docile. In mice, testosterone induces fighting behavior.

Those centers of the brain which control the emotions do not react solely to testosterone, however. Estrogen and progestin, hormones whose levels change with the menstrual cycle, can induce a number of physiological changes other than uterine, and an even greater degree of psychological change.

Changes in hormone levels are responded to more severely by some women than by others; and, from month to month, experiential differences also tend to vary. Immediately prior to menstruation, some women experience mental depression, mood swings, headaches, and changes in vision. With the accumulation of tissue fluid in the organs affected, swelling and stiffness of the hands and feet may occur, and contact lenses suddenly may not fit. Impairment of visual tracking is reported by some advanced players, while others experience impairment of general coordination. For some women, on the other hand, these secondary effects of menstruation are negligible.

The superior flexibility of women may well be under hormonal influence. During the late stages of pregnancy, there is a loosening of the joints of the pelvic girdle; and in nongravid states, if large doses of estrogen are administered, one of the side effects is the stretching of joint ligaments. Change from female to male posture occurs in those endocrine disturbances in which women produce excess testosterone, with the angulation of the forearm to the upper arm becoming "masculine." These changes are reversed with the restoration of the proper estrogen-testosterone ratio. It therefore seems not unlikely that estrogen-testosterone ratios also are involved in the extensibility of females' joints, in the absence of pregnancy and pathology.

Marked changes in hormone levels occur in pregnancy, and apparently bring with them transient impairment of coordination. Pregnancy can cause nausea and general "sickness" on the tennis court, just as it can anywhere else. Childbirth can apparently accomplish the opposite: some women feel that having a child led to an improvement in their game. Here, too, experiences vary. Bea Hilton, a strong amateur player, found that during pregnancy she did exceptionally well at tennis, golf, and skiing, and that after delivery her concentration was better and her tennis game sharper. She attributes the improvement to a more stable and relaxed life. Margaret Court found that she could get into top physical condition much faster after her son Danny was born. In addition, she felt that she was much less tense during matches. In 1973, at thirty years of age, new mother Margaret did in almost everyone on the Virginia Slims tour and most of her opponents in other tournaments around the world, winning more than $200,000 in prize money.

The psychological factor of self-fulfillment may be one reason for improved performance after pregnancy; a second factor may be physiological. It is known that there are endocrine differences before and after pregnancy, and although it is not known how these hormonal changes might improve performance, the possibility of a connection is definitely there.

Until recently, the statistics said "Advantage women" in terms of two major stress-related diseases: heart attacks and ulcers. Protection against coronary artery disease was specifically ascribed to estrogen, while protection against duodenal ulcer was ascribed to nonparticipation in the testosterone-ridden world of making a living. The medical community was certain that women were more resistant to stress than were men, while everyone in the sports establishment was certain of women's lesser resistance.

It is now evident that hormones cannot provide the entire story. The increase in the number of women in competitive middle- and upper-echelon business and professional positions has been accompanied by an increase in stress-related illnesses among women. In the world of professional tennis, where environmental change is rapid and competition is continuous, women and men do equally well or poorly against the tides of stress. The Slims tour, a certain qualifier for nomination as a world-class stress test, provides even further evidence that women can withstand the rigors of professional sports.

Reaction Time

Reaction time is faster in men than in women. This is an empirical fact; but no one seems to be sure of the exact reasons or the biological mechanisms involved.

It is known that the rate of females' nerve impulse transmission is identical to that of males, as are the regulation of carbohydrate metabolism and the production of adrenalin and cortisone. Both males and females experience variations in biological rhythms, their cycles occurring on daily, seasonal, and biennial or triennial bases; and they are equally disturbed by changes in their accustomed daily routines. It seems evident that here, too, hormones cannot tell the whole story.

It is conjectured that one important reason for men's more rapid reaction time is their superior training. Repetitive use under maximal effort has an immense influence on all the physical qualities needed in sports. Reaction time, intensity and speed of muscle contraction, coordination, and timing all need training. For many reasons, the athletic training of men and women has been not just separate but unequal. Until recently, in almost all sports, women's teams were not well coached; women did not train as hard as men, and seldom tested the upper limits of their abilities.

It is known that physiological responses to exercise training are similar in women and men. Fat indices are reduced; tolerance for minimal work, as measured by lactic acid accumulation during exercise, is increased; maximal oxygen uptake (a measure of endurance) is increased; and heart rate for a given degree of moderate exercise (mean work heart rate) is decreased.

The major role of training cannot be denied. Those females who either train with males or follow training programs identical to those of men turn themselves into clearly superior physical products. After the 1972 Olympics, for example, the East German swimming team trained its men and women identically. The following year, in the World Championships at Belgrade, the German girls took ten of the fourteen events and set seven world records. The sheer "skin" suit was claimed as a factor; but the following year the American girls wore it against the East Germans, and the East Germans won nevertheless. In track and field, Maren Seidler, the top U.S. shot putter, attributes her continued improvement to training with her male counterparts.

Dominating women's tennis for many years, Margaret Court has stood apart from other women players. She was held in awe by her colleagues not so much for her record as for her training techniques. She did road work for speed and stamina, used weights to strengthen her arms and shoulders, and frequently worked out at a gym in Melbourne.

At John Gardiner's ranch—where, as at some other tennis camps, students are grouped on the basis of ability—the small groups are frequently integrated and the men and women are drilled equally hard. Virginia Wade approves, feeling that when women train and play together with men, they improve their game. Tougher training and competition bring about better performance, for women as well as men.

Psychosocial Factors

Basic physical and functional differences exist between men and women, but these differences are not large. They cannot, by themselves, account for the spread between male and female performance records. It therefore follows that psychosocial or psychocultural factors must be at work.

Sex-stratified attitudes, beliefs, and modes of functioning help determine not just who wins or loses but how the game is played. Learned behavior, learned "reasons" for that behavior, and learned belief in the sanctity and efficacy of those "reasons" are all acquired in the process of socialization. Their power and tenacity cannot be overestimated.

The majority of women believe that they *cannot* be what they have been taught they *must not* be: all the things it takes to function adequately in the world—determined, hard working, tough, aggressive, and when the situation calls for it, overtly hostile—in short, "unfeminine."

And taught to lose, the majority of women do as they have been taught.

Origins and inequities

Conformity to culturally assigned sex roles begins with names and the colors pink and blue. It continues with sex-stratified toys, clothing, and games selected by sexist adults; with the degree and type of activity and exploration of the environment condoned by sexist adults; with the amount of food one can get away with eating or not eating; with how dirty one can get and how much one is allowed to scream, cry, throw, and hit; and with being conditioned not only to give but to believe the acceptable answers to that dreary question which adults seem compelled to ask, "What do you want to be when you grow up?"

School-age boys can spend their free time on the sandlots or in Little League; but most little girls are shielded from contact sports, being made to take music or dance lessons instead. To ensure that a woman's place will not be on the playing fields, girls have been taught the importance of attempting to attain the societal norms of "beauty" and "proportion."

Women vs. Men

Athletics and femininity have been considered mutually antagonistic. Until the early 1970s, sports had a universal aura of masculinity. While top male athletes appeared in a wide variety of advertising—the inference being that great dollops of masculinity would be conferred on the user of the product advertised—Madison Avenue went principally to Hollywood and fashion models for their examples of femininity, never to women in sports.

There are high school boys' teams in all the major sports, and in selected minor ones; but there are still few girls' teams. The budget allocations for male and female sports continue to be in different galaxies. Until recently, the extraordinary male athlete was offered scholarships to attend college, but the female athlete who excelled despite the cultural hurdles was offered none. As late as 1973, only about 50 women in the United States held athletic scholarships, compared with some 50,000 men.

If the female athlete survived the pressures of society, the paucity of training programs, and the near impossibility of becoming a professional athlete, there was still a face-down ace in the establishment hand: to treat her with "kindness" and "understanding," to demand less than the rigors of male training from her.

The male mystique is no longer holding, and tradition in sports may be going the way of tradition in life. In 1972, Title IX of the Educational Amendments Act established the legal basis for equality in college athletics. In 1973, Billie Jean King beat Bobby Riggs in the most publicized match of all time. While her sisters were making breakthroughs in many traditionally male-only sports, she went on almost singlehandedly to achieve equality in tournament prize money for men and women.

Many of the inequities in women's versus men's sports can be legislated away, but it will take more than laws to change

Bobby Riggs giving a congratulatory kiss to Billie Jean King after Ms. King took three straight sets in their $100,000 winner-take-all match in the Houston Astrodome.

attitudes. Billie Jean King and girls' Little League teams notwithstanding, active participation in sports still does not constitute generally acceptable, full-time female behavior. Instead, it tends to be seen as a fleeting aberration, a hobby, a little something to do until settling down to the real business of female life, or a way of "keeping one's figure."

But Ms. King is simply not the girl next door. Rather, she is a fluke, a star—this generation's equivalent of what used to be produced by the motion picture industry. As one nonplayer conjectures, "Everybody knows her husband handles the business end of her career. There's nothing the girl really has to do except dash from one place to the other playing tennis all day. Maybe what really happened was she had a pushy mother. That's usually what makes girls act that way.

Whatever it was, you can be sure something odd or unusual happened back there, somewhere."

Hunters and Warriors

There is still plenty of male chauvinism around, despite Billie Jean King's victory over Bobby Riggs. In athletics, many men—probably the majority—cannot lose to a woman without sustaining some degree of psychic injury. Any woman who plays a strong game of tennis can cite numerous firsthand examples.

The sportsman's need to beat a woman competitor borders on compulsion. When a woman tennis professional does have the ability to trounce any average male player, the chauvinists turn pragmatic, challenging her to a related sport—paddleball, Ping Pong, or badminton. At the same time that men cannot bear losing to a woman, they do not consider it much of an achievement to defeat her. Somehow, if it is to be serious, competition must be man against man.

This attitude is doubtless a calling forth of that ancient, now romanticized facet of "masculine" psychology, the hunter and warrior—the idea that men are forever having to work off their "natural" or "instinctual" aggressiveness because they are "by nature" hunters and warriors. The concept does have prehistoric roots; and since natural selection may have emphasized such a genotype, perhaps it has some genetic basis as well. But more likely it is merely a culturally sanctioned excuse upon which some would prefer to confer genetic status.

The caves and graves of anthropological reality reveal the much adored hunters and warriors to have been flea-bitten, worm-infested, greased, painted, and scared youngsters. Is this really the average male tennis player, cleaned up, dressed up, racket in hand, but still so man-to-man aggressive that he never has to get psyched up?

The propensity toward certain types of behavior may, in

part, be genetically determined. Some infant males, for example, are reported to be more negatively aggressive and exploratory than some infant females. But it is highly doubtful that the propensity to hold specific attitudes can be genetic in origin. Where is the cold, unassailable proof that it can be? In the wistful desire for "male bonding"? In the imprints of the graylag goose? In the supposed psyches of extinct apes? In the tall, blond, blue-eyed Master Race, perhaps?

Male and Female Stereotypes

Passivity is the behavioral mode central to what is popularly classified as "feminine." Femininity is a manner of perceiving oneself, the external world, and one's relationship to it which is manifested in patterns of behavior which are reactive rather than active, receptive rather than acquisitive, renunciative rather than assertive. Feminine behavior involves the renunciation of active drives, the sacrificing of one's own assertiveness and potential attainments, the submersion of one's life so that another might live better, the vicarious experiencing of one's life through the activities of another—usually, one's mate.

Since the submersion of the self can never be entire, the conflicts which women experience concerning their femininity center around the gap between their naturally active and assertive tendencies and the socially sanctioned, learned, internalized rules of the game concerning what a "real" female is like, i.e., reactive, receptive, and renunciative. No woman in this generation is totally free of the conflict; and it is probable that few if any of them have completely resolved it. Even driving, cool-headed females in the midst of successful careers still experience panicky moments when confronted with the necessity of having to decide, to act, to compete.

The "fear of success" investigation by Matina Horner provides insights into the dynamics underlying the relative lack of achievement among women. The findings of this 1969 study of female college students add up to one thing: Young women want what they learn to want, and fear what they learn to fear. Consequently, they develop attitudes and patterns of behavior which will lead them away from what they fear and toward what they do not fear.

Horner divided her sample into two groups: those having a strong fear of success and those with little fear of it. A comparison of the attitudes held by each group revealed that a strong fear of success will lead a female college student to conform to the conventional societal attitudes that women should either be in the home or, if in business, in positions not competitive with men. Conversely, the subsample possessing relatively little fear of success revealed attitudes and patterns of behavior similar to those of male high-achievers, e.g., they performed better in competition than when working alone. This study supports the conclusion that the desire to fail cannot be part of the psychophysiological equipment one is born with. It must involve learned behavior.

For the most part, the stereotype of women as emotional beings is the result of their culturally sanctioned freedom to express their emotions. It is probable that men have emotions similar, if not identical, to those of women; but it is difficult to tell since, from early childhood, most males are subjected to consistent and at times brutal training by parents, coaches, siblings, and peers, all aimed at repressing emotional expression. The expressionless face is masculine. Silence is masculine. So is brute strength.

But it goes beyond that, for even the manner in which emotion is acceptably expressed is sex-stratified. The passive expression of both positive and negative emotion is considered feminine. Tears, sullenness, the passive denial of sexual favors, sweet smiles and subdued laughter, forgiveness and forbearance are what is expected from women. Providing they do not scream too loudly, tear only their own hair, and smash the dishes rather than take an ax to the furniture, they can get away with a tantrum once in a while. They may slap, but they must not punch. They are supposed to be weak.

The active expression of negative emotion—anger, rage, overt manifestations of basic hostility—is considered masculine.

The degree to which the passive-active distinction between male and female behavior has been incorporated and sanctioned in both male and female psyches is illustrated by the results of a study comparing the sexes on the exhibition of instrumental (doing) versus expressive (saying) traits and on feelings of dependence versus independence. In general, the women saw themselves as being more expressive than instrumental in orientation; they considered expressive traits to relate to independence rather than dependence. They felt that the mark of independence was to engage in talk and not action. The men, on the other hand, saw themselves as being more instrumental than expressive; they associated independence with instrumental traits and with the suppression of expressive ones. They thought of the strong, silent, active type as being the independent man.

Athletics has always been considered the embodiment of instrumental rather than expressive behavior. The athlete—even the woman athlete—was strong and silent. However, in the era of Nastase, Connors, and tennis on television, a gradual change in this attitude is unmistakably evident. Compared to "what the players are getting away with today," the volatile Dennis Ralston considers his own behavior in the previous decade to have been exemplary.

The change is not extreme, though. The flamboyance of Nastase and the crassness of Connors are considered well within the realm of masculine behavior. And rather than being seen as some of the sillier manifestations of hostile, infantile, egocentric personalities of either gender, their behavior tends to be excused as being, at worst, merely transient eccentricity on the part of proven males. An aggressive, successful style of play is still considered masculine; Billie Jean King is still said to play a "man's game."

Until recently, aggressiveness in women athletes was equated almost universally with masculinity. But this has also been the lot of women in medicine, law, and any rank in business higher than assistant or Girl Friday—in short, anywhere where assertive, competitive action must take place in the open. Such women have tended to be considered by members of both sexes as masculine, lesbian, or "castrating."

The assertive nature of tennis has not kept millions of women from taking to the courts. But this is because tennis provides a sanctioned, ritualized outlet for aggression; as a game, it tends to be seen as outside the province of real life. One woman we interviewed said that if people thought her feminine as a woman and aggressive as a tennis player, they would sit up and take notice. She would like that, she said. But how much chance does she have of being positively perceived as *both* a feminine and an aggressive woman in the real world?

The need to be assertive in tennis has functioned to prevent millions of women from being winning players, causing them psychic conflict and physical fear to a sometimes disturbing degree. Take Sheila, for example. Sheila is a teacher. She is young and feminine. There is little inhibition in her tennis style; she plays a spirited game. When it is appropriate, she will rush the net; she has no fear of being hit. She thinks of assertiveness in terms of winning the game or match, rather than as a style of play. But Sheila is possessed by a conflict between her femininity and any assertive role she may play. Off court, she had always considered herself nonassertive. Then she discovered that others did not share her self-assessment. Meanwhile, on court, she found that winning against a male brought this conflict to a state of acute awareness. Now she is working out the problem of equating assertiveness with the seeking of one's own rights, needs, and desires. She is trying to convince her emotional self that assertiveness is neither masculine nor feminine.

The Question of Risk

Although the avoidance of risk-taking is neither genetically nor physiologically determined, for almost all women the prospect of extreme challenge and risk produces fear rather than stimulation. Few well-conditioned women are adventurous, let alone daring.

As usual, Billie Jean King's life has been an exception. In her tennis game she often goes for the more difficult shot. Just being a woman professional was risky business until 1972, and Billie Jean was in her prime in 1966 and 1967. Risky, too, at their inception were the women's professional tour, World Team Tennis, and *women Sports* magazine.

Nevertheless, venturesome women are rare. It is the men who set the speed records in planes, boats, cars, and on skis—none of which requires great physical strength. Moreover, men were the first to take the risks necessary to cross oceans in balloons, small planes, and on rafts, all feats that women were physically capable of achieving.

Fear of physical injury is almost universal among women, and is a major motivation for risk-avoidance. Although women who are well trained and conditioned should have no greater fear of injury than do their male counterparts, women players at the net tend to feel threatened by overheads and drives from close in. They will turn away from the shot and duck, often before the opponent has struck the ball.

Fear of personal injury even affects many of the women tennis professionals. Chris Evert has been known to experience occasional apprehension as to possible physical injury. In one tournament, the Pacific Southwest Open, it was a female *official* who exhibited this fear. A close call went against the doubles team of Erik Van Dillen and Dick Stockton. Erik complained to the umpire, "Tell her not to duck her head when she makes a call."

Women vs. Men

"All you do is hit them in the chest if you can, and they back off," Arthur Ashe once told a television interviewer, in describing how women can be intimidated in mixed doubles. Ashe noted, however, that Margaret Court, Evonne Goolagong, and Virginia Wade could not be intimidated; he might also have cited Billie Jean King and Martina Navratilova. Ashe's controversial statement brought a deluge of letters from irate women. One male tennis player, who defended Ashe's strategy in the name of sexual equality, had his letter answered by a female player who told of her counterstrategy of aiming for a male opponent's groin.

Self-Image

Positive correlations exist between self-image and feelings of physical adequacy, in both men and women. Apprehension as to the consequences of being adventurous, of taking risks, of exposing oneself to possible injury, of doing rather than saying, of being aggressive rather than passive—all these are manifestations of a fragile, constricted concept of the self, a learned belief in one's "innate" vulnerability and fundamental inadequacy to deal with the challenges of the outside world.

The adequacy of men's bodies is judged primarily in terms of physical performance, while the adequacy of women's bodies is judged on quite a different continuum. As yet, not even many feminists consider a woman's body in terms of grace, rhythm, speed, or athletic performance. Say the word "body" to a feminist, and her first association is most likely to be in one of two categories: uterus, abortion, the "Pill," and IUDs; or the male view of the female body as sex object.

One's body is one's most immediate environment. If we are not secure in our bodies, what can we expect of our relationships to the rest of our surroundings?

An adequate self-image can lead to enjoyment of one's body in motion. Most men have experienced the exuberance which can accompany athletic activity. Most women have not.

Looking Ahead

Once upon a time, there seemed little question as to what constituted psychological maleness and femaleness. Now the issue is considerably more problematic. While attitudes concerning sex-differentiated social roles are becoming less rigid, the change is not rapid and the desire for change by no means universal.

Many individuals, including a good number of psychiatrists, both male and female, feel that with the exception of primary reproductive functions, there should be no sex-coded societal roles whatsoever. This attitude continues to be rejected by the majority of women, a phenomenon not without precedent. A skimming of Southern history reveals that a certain percentage of manumitted slaves chose to remain with their masters; the ancient Greeks were well aware that there would always be some prisoners who had learned to love their chains.

Integration of men's and women's sports programs continues to meet a great deal of resistance from the sports establishment, and there is still a widespread reluctance on the part of women to work and play as equals with men. They prefer the security of their all-female groups.

Despite their slower game, the women tennis pros have convinced the promoters, as well as themselves, that they can draw the crowds as well as the men can. They argue that the spectators can more closely identify with their slower game, and that a fan who is a weekend player cannot imagine playing against the power of the top men.

Not only is such a hypothesis open to question, but it also

runs contrary to the entire superathlete phenomenon that is American sports today. The fans do not visualize themselves in the shoes of Pelé, Seaver, Jabbar, and Ali. They come in great numbers to see the stars in action. To say that spectators can more closely identify with second-rate players is analogous to the comments of Senator Roman Hruska after Richard Nixon nominated G. Harrold Carswell to fill a vacancy on the Supreme Court. Everyone else decried Carswell's lack of legal stature and scholarship, but Senator Hruska said, "There are a lot of mediocre people, and they are entitled to a little representation, aren't they?"

How much the gap in records can close is still conjectural. Women must first be allowed to become seriously interested in sports. They should be trained to use—and allow themselves to use—athletic activity as a valid avenue of active emotional expression. They should know the pride of athletic accomplishment. They should have the peak experience of reaching the very limits of physical possibility, and sometimes even a glimpse beyond.

Our attitudes that certain sports are masculine and certain others feminine must change. We must recognize that the exploration of physical possibility is not limited by gender. This means that girls should play stickball as well as house. Boys should learn how to jump double Dutch as well as play touch tackle. (In tennis, where footwork is a vital factor, double-Dutch jump-rope training would be an especially good idea.) Poor and disadvantaged boys have long had the chance to escape a financially preordained life of hardship by winning athletic scholarships. Girls should have the same opportunity.

Good coaches cost more than mediocre ones; but if women's teams on the college level and women athletes on the professional level can attract the fans, the money will be there. How many Americans even knew what soccer was until Pelé appeared on the scene?

In addition, women will have to shape up, get out there, and get themselves up to first-class standards. If they are content merely to express their outrage at the male chauvinist sports establishment, we are back to the expressive vs. instrumental concept of femininity/masculinity, and the MCPs will be reinforced in their view that women are all talk and no action.

The fourth estate has already seen the light. In December 1976, *Sports Illustrated* not only honored Chris Evert as Athlete of the Year but also considered women for most of the runner-up positions.

To sum up: Actual, purposive differences do exist between males and females. In tennis, these physiological distinctions evidence themselves in strength of serve and return, and in reaction time. The other differences which exist between men and women are an impure and mutable amalgam of the societal, the cultural, and the psychological. In tennis, these implied differences evidence themselves principally in degree of expressed aggression and, ultimately, in the difference between doing what one has to do in order to win versus doing what one can get away with in order to lose.

Sports have taken a leading role in changing persistent sex-role stereotypes. Many sports emphasize grace and form, both supposed characteristics of femininity. Yet male gymnasts, divers, tennis players, and other sportsmen exhibit grace and form and are no less masculine for it. Conversely, daring and endurance are allegedly masculine characteristics. Yet female gymnasts on the balance beam and uneven parallel bars seemingly defy physical laws and human possibility; and women swim the English Channel and around Manhattan Island in defiance of tides, temperature, and exhaustion. These athletes are often the most feminine of women in their other roles.

Male-female differences that have been imposed on us by cultural and psychological determinants may evaporate when they follow sports into the sunshine of a free spirit.

CHAPTER ELEVEN

Winding Down

WHY do you sometimes feel exhausted and depressed when the match is over? Part of the answer lies in the nervous system, which is equally chemical and electrical in nature. Where nerves are most concentrated—in the brain—the concentration of their chemical mediators is greatest.

Alteration in the levels of three of these neurotransmission agents—the amines norepinephrine, dopamine, and serotonin —are intimately involved in disturbances of emotional and behavioral states. Along with adrenalin (epinephrine), norepinephrine also influences cardiac output. Stability of brain function depends on the maintenance of proper amine levels. Not only are the emotional stresses of daily life contained in this way, but optimum performance in sporting events is achieved as well.

Amines are manufactured in the brain by amino acids carried there by the bloodstream. They are released in the synapse and then for the most part deactivated by the metabolic processes of oxidation and methylation. They are in a constant state of change, being formed, mobilized, inactivated, and/or returned to their original site, with the entire process being repeated again and again. Not only is their synthesis complex, requiring two or three steps and a specific enzyme at each step, but there are also ten or more influences on the rate at which they are formed, and several additional influences on their rate and style of deactivation. A lot is happening on a great many levels, and much can go wrong.

Just what constitutes a proper amine level is not presently known; accurate predictions as to whether, at any given time, the amine level of any individual will be optimal or less than adequate cannot presently be made. What is known is that, along with age, endocrine activity, and diet, amine synthesis is influenced by competition and stress. Excessive competition and stress, whether in business, at school, or on the tennis courts, can lead not only to inhibition of learning and memory but also to exhaustion and emotional depression.

Competition and Stress

An athlete practicing or competing at or near maximal levels mobilizes larger amounts of norepinephrine and epinephrine. This can be measured by the amount of breakdown product (metabolite) appearing in the urine. Competitive athletic activity significantly increases urinary excretion of catecholamine metabolites, even though the calories expended may be the same as during practice. The additional psychological factors involved in competition provide the difference.

Chronic exhaustion in sports is not only a physical condition but an emotional one as well. The combined factors result in the depletion of norepinephrine stores. This chemical deficiency inhibits winning ways. Losing (especially in tennis) then drives the chemically depressed psyche down a level further toward despair.

In sports, repeated physical activity at or near maximal levels can produce stress; and the line separating peak condition from overtraining and exhaustion is a narrow one. Environmental stress (such as drugs, diet, and extreme heat and cold) and psychophysiological stress (such as competitive overexertion) can deplete amine stores. The body's normal reaction to low amine levels is to increase the rate of synthesis; but if stress becomes long-term, it is conceivable that metabolic breakdown will lead to chronically low levels of the biogenic amines.

In the last few years, several top tennis professionals have been subject to the overuse stress syndrome. The lure of prize money and the proliferation of tournaments have attracted many of them to continuous competition. It is not unusual for a player to compete in two tournaments simultaneously. In 1974, Bjorn Borg, competing in both the W.C.T. Championships and Davis Cup play, flew over from a Davis Cup match in Warsaw and beat Rod Laver in a grueling, spectacular semifinal match which lasted five sets. The next day, in the final, Borg played well for three sets but completely wilted in the fourth, winning only a single game and a few points. Ilie Nastase experienced a more chronic exhaustion from his incessant competition in 1972 and 1973. He continued for the forty-plus weeks of tournament play per year into 1974, but his exhaustion was evident in his poor record that year.

Wilhelm Reich's theory of "bodily armor"—the concept that an individual's neuromuscular systems can become rigid, or "armored," in response to psychological conflicts and anxieties—is of special pertinence to the athlete. Even a slight imbalance in posture, one of Reich's prime signs, can restrict the fluidity of one's swing. To choose one example, Stan Smith after being ranked Number One in the nation suddenly saw his game decline a couple of levels. He went from being the scourge of the courts to holding a most unenviable record: fifteen months of losses. It all began about the time of his marriage. Although many factors were undoubtedly involved, any small tensions between marriage and tennis must have contributed to Smith's early losses. The additional element of defeat nurturing defeat subsequently reinforced the original factors.

Excessive motivation to win can lead the player to ignore the fact that muscles, tendons, ligaments, and bone are mortal, and to call upon his body to do more than he would ask of a machine. In effect, he counters its warning signals with the equivalent of "Shut up and keep playing!" General exhaustion is only one possible consequence of this motivation-dominated behavior. When the body is pressed beyond its limits, the cardiovascular system and the metabolic mechanisms can collapse entirely.

Those who do not heed the fact that a muscle is not reacting optimally may be surprised by one of the common sports injuries, caused by too forceful or overly protracted use. The ligaments of the joints, the Achilles tendon, and the muscles of the legs are all vulnerable to overuse problems. Inflammation, tears, and complete rupture may occur, and stress fractures are no rarity. Such injuries are often associated with underlying structural weakness, but overuse stress deals the final blow.

Individual muscle weakness raises an additional psycho-physiological problem. If a weakness exists in a muscle which would ordinarily be used for certain movements, unconventional motor patterns may develop. Other muscles adaptively take up the slack, a habit is established, and the weak muscle remains weak. Such individual muscle weakness may exist in an otherwise well-trained athlete.

Working independently, Leo Burkett of San Diego State College and Joseph Zohar of New York have shown that many recurrent hamstring muscle tears result from such muscle imbalance. While quantitatively measuring the strength of various leg muscle groups of several athletes, they noted certain cases of muscle imbalance and consequently were able to predict with a high degree of accuracy which athletes would suffer muscle pulls in the weeks ahead.

It goes without saying that an individual weak muscle must be discovered before it can be strengthened. A history of previous injury to a specific muscle is a good indication of residual weakness. Physiological testing can be done as well. Once a weak muscle is found, exercises must be designed specifically for that muscle. This principle applies to tennis players as to other athletes.

Depression

There are two major types of depression which the athlete tends to suffer, transient and clinical. To varying degrees, three basic factors are at work in each.

Causes of Depression

We have already examined the first factor, exhaustion. The second is age. With advancing age, there is increased activity of monamine oxidase, an enzyme which oversees oxidation—one of the metabolic processes which breaks down the biogenic amines. The resultant lowered amine stores find statistical expression in the increased incidence of depression after middle age.

The third factor is related to identity and self-worth. The depleting effect of injury or illness on identity was shown in a British psychiatric study of neurosis in athletic and nonathletic middle-aged men. In the case of the nonathletic sample members, neurosis was related to impairment of life: poor interpersonal relationships, traumatic childhoods, and un-happy marriages. In the athlete-neurotics, such background factors differed little from those of the general population. Acute situational stress, rather than a pervasive, cumulative psychic immobilization, precipitated the onset of neurotic ill-ness. In almost three-quarters of these cases, the causal factor was an injury or illness which threatened the physical prowess of the individual and, hence, the integrity of his self-image. The agents of stress included fractures, concussion, influenza, and coronary occlusion. The stresses were sometimes cumula-tive; often, a single occurrence was sufficient.

Types of Depression

Transient or mood depression occurs after the match—especially if one loses. The low mood experienced after losing is not a pathological state. The feeling is not intractable; the individual can still function, even though, for a time, the world does not seem too pleasant.

Although it usually occurs in individuals whose primary motivation in tennis is winning, low mood level can also occur in players whose caliber of play has fallen below normal. If he then proceeds to practice harder, or seeks out and beats a different opponent, or wins at something else, or beats the same opponent on another day, his depression "goes away."

Athletic "staleness" and some types of clinical psychiatric depression are similar in their symptoms and possibly in their chemistry. Athletic exhaustion is characterized by persistent soreness and stiffness, nervousness, a drop in performance, pessimism, insomnia, and loss of appetite. Psychiatric depres-sion is also attended by at least these last three symptoms. Neither form of depression is likely to just "go away."

Depression has been considered a specific type of behavior for over 2,000 years. Hippocrates described it as "melan-cholia" and noted the disorder's manic-depressive character. The ancient Greek physicians were fairly accurate in their

A photograph of a crestfallen Virginia Wade, taken after her defeat by Olga Morozova in the 1974 Wimbledon semi-finals, illustrates the letdown that often follows the loss of a prized match. Miss Wade, nonetheless, bounced back to win the Wimbledon crown in 1977.

description of clinical depression. Neither the condition nor its symptoms have really changed. Insomnia, loss of appetite, loss of libido, lowered self-esteem, bouts of deep sadness, tears, a generally pessimistic outlook, and loss of a sense of humor still afflict a significant segment of humanity.

Frontiers of Research

Considerable knowledge concerning the particulars of depressive states has been accumulated over the past twenty-five years. Much of it contains implications for athletics.

Individuals in a state of clinical depression tend to complain of cognitive inefficiency and lowered motor performance. Interest in, or patience for, problem-solving and other forms of involved thought is diminished, and even everyday activities are performed with sluggishness and great effort.

While it previously had been assumed that psychomotor inhibition was a sine qua non of depression, a number of studies done during the 1950s and 1960s in the fields of experimental and clinical psychology resulted in contrary findings. Although depressed patients had a low estimation of their abilities, their *actual* performance in various psychomotor test situations was unimpaired. Even reaction time was normal. Another study found that depressed patients withstood fatigue as well as nondepressed individuals did. However, there is an effect on spatial perception. Depression and impairment of distance discrimination seem to be related, and the height of a horizontal plane is often estimated inaccurately. The implications of this finding for tennis are more than academic.

A study investigating the influence of success and failure on task performance found that success improved the subsequent performance of depressed patients, while failure improved that of the nondepressed—although repeated failure and resultant loss of confidence may cause anxiety even in those situations which the individual ordinarily handles successfully.

Concurrently with the above studies, biochemists discovered that clinical depression was accompanied by changes in brain levels of the biogenic amines—those same fascinating chemical mediators which bring equilibrium to the well-adjusted player. And endocrinologists found that the same physiological changes which regularly accompany stress also occur in depression, in direct proportion to its severity. It was also found that other physiological changes can accompany psychological stress. The helplessness and hopelessness characteristic of depression often results from an accumulation of psychophysiologically stressful life events.

Much work has been done regarding the mechanism of emotional change and the somatic effects of such change. Much remains to be done. Research efforts in neurobiochemistry, endocrine metabolism, and in the study of the "giving up" syndrome have been impressive in establishing definite relationships between changes in body and in mind; but the chicken-egg question has yet to be resolved. We must remember that concomitant events may or may not be causally related, and that even when a cause-effect relationship does appear to exist, it is often very difficult to tell with any degree of accuracy which is which.

Fighting Depression

We have seen the detrimental effects of athletic staleness on the body, the mind, and the scorecard. The athlete has a few ways out of the trap. If the cause is excessive physical activity—playing too hard and too frequently over a long span of time—the solution is rest and a change of environment.

At the end of 1976, for example, Bob Lutz felt the crumbles coming on. He took a two-month vacation, swimming and surfing on the Pacific coast. Then, in February 1977, he played in the Ocean City International Tournament and beat top-seeded Guillermo Vilas in the semifinals.

Athletic depression may also be caused by a string of losses which are not related to physiological exhaustion. The problem may be defective form and stroke production. If so, the player may need someone else's sharp eyes to spot the deficiency. Perhaps, too, his placements are leaving too little margin for error.

If, on the other hand, athletic depression is based on anxiety and outside emotional factors, the player should look beyond his game for the cause of the problem and its solution. Whether the causes are intrapsychic or situational, the individual is often too close to himself or his surroundings to make an accurate assessment. Coaches, trainers, and physicians who are sensitive and aware often can be more objective. The athlete can then start back on the victory road.

CHAPTER TWELVE

Afterword

MANY factors affect the game of tennis. For the serious player, a recognition of the power of these factors can serve as an agent of change. Improvement may be slow and erratic but, with perseverance, it never fails to appear.

As individuals, we often think of the cognitive factors as immutable parts of our makeup:

"I'm just not an organized person."

"I simply cannot concentrate."

"Decisions, decisions. Pour me a drink, and *you* decide."

There is nothing difficult about analytic thought. Given the proper information, the cortex does most of it for you. Intense and protracted concentration can be learned. Decision-making can be quite automatic, provided, once again, that the cortex has the information.

Tennis provides an opportunity to put all of our psychological efforts into an activity that is separate and distinct from all the stress-producing events and people in everyday life. If the outside world of emotional ups and downs can be put aside, both psyche and tennis game stand to benefit. Our emotions and even our personalities are not so rigid that they are immutable.

We all have more flexibility than we give ourselves credit for. We can modify and fine-tune psychological traits. With enough will and work, the most detrimental of psychological factors can always be tempered. Like adversity, such liabilities can even be turned to advantage.

In addition, we can develop our fitness for tennis so that strengths can more than compensate for weaknesses. And we can sharpen our tactical facilities by having a variety of shots in our armory, by gaining the experience of many matches and tournaments, and by giving thought and study to general strategies and specific tactics.

There is indeed a formula for each of us, but it cannot be a magic one. It must be as complex and individual as each of us is complex and unique. These pages hold some of its ingredients.

The way to the formula in tennis is by examining the myriad factors presented earlier, and by combining them with hours and hours of playing, observation, and analysis. The critical eye must examine physical abilities and strategic skills, along with motivation, perception, learning, and all the other facets of psychophysiological function. Finally, the way to excellence must be custom-designed.

What psychology can do for tennis is only half of the tennis-psychology cycle. The other half is what tennis can do for the psyche.

At all levels of the game, tennis can contribute to a feeling of well-being, a sense of personal accomplishment and self-worth. Tennis can be the antitoxin to the irritations of every-day. The alchemy of tennis can turn physical effort and motion into joy. There are the special ties which develop between doubles partners. There is the euphoria of the days when the ball always hits the "sweet spot" on the racket strings, when every shot can be willed to the inside edge of the chalk line.

And best of all, there is that once in a while when, in a flash of heightened performance—that special gift for persistence—one gets a glimpse of what lies beyond.

Sweet victory (àla Bobby Riggs).

WIDE WORLD PHOTO

INDEX

Accentuation in perception, 55
Acclimatization: to altitude, 97; in-game, 102; perception and, 53–54
Adams, R. D., 139
Aerobic metabolism, 45–47
Aggression: dominant-submissive relationship and, 124, 125; forms of, 15–18; hunters and warriors and, 147–48; motivation and, 13–15; in tennis personality, 83–84
Alan King-Caesar's Palace tournament, 125
Alcohol, effects of, 90
Ali, Muhammed, 155
Altitude, coping with, 96–97
Amine levels: and depression after middle age, 161; importance of, 157, 158
Anaerobic metabolism, 45–47
Analytic thought: as type of learning, 63–64
Anxiety, 26–33; causes of, 30–33; as essential, 7; as foe of concen-tration, 39; level of precompeti-tion, 84–85; relaxation to re-duce, *see* Relaxation; warmup, 84–90
Ardrey, Robert, 16, 17
Arousal stage: altering levels of, 30; of awakeness, 27–28; influ-ence of, on memory, 57–58; levels of, 28–30; in warmup, 84–90
Ashe, Arthur, 4, 32; concentration of, 34; continual variation used by, 103; and court personality of opponents, 80; dominance by, 127; in doubles play, 107; and gamesmanship of oppo-nents, 116; on intimidating women, 153; precompetition arousal in, 85; situational cre-ativity of, 74; speed of serve of, 53; on staying loose, 37
Assessment: and readiness as as-pects of warmup, 77; in warmup, 79–84
Association: learning by, 61–62

Goolagong, Evonne, *see* Cawley,
Evonne Goolagong
Graebner, Carole Caldwell, 37;
and dominance by King, 127;
and mixed doubles, 111; tennis
personality of, 83
Graebner, Clark: and mixed doubles, 111; and Nastase gamesmanship, 116
Grand Slam finals (1977), 100

Haywood, Spencer, 85–86
Heart rate, 44; high environmen-
tal temperatures and, 95; sex
and, 93
Heat: coping with, 95–96
Heightened anxiety: defined, 31
Hilton, Bea: childbirth and im-
provement in game of, 141
Hippocrates, 163
Holistic method of learning, 68–
69
Hopman, Harry: and lobbing
into the sun, 105
Hormones: sex differences in,
138–42
Horner, Matina, 148–49
Hruska, Roman, 155
Humidity: coping with, 95–96

Identity: defined, 10–11; depres-
sion and, 161–62
Illumination: in creative process,
73
Incubation: in creative process,
73
Inhibition: anxiety and, 31
Inner Game of Tennis, The (Gall-
way), 87
In-game, 98–111; applying psy-

chology in, 100–4; exploiting
opponent's weaknesses in, 104–
6; rules of strategy in, 98–100;
tips for doubles, 106–11
"in" players, 122–24
Inspiration: in creative process,
73
Intelligence, 75
Ismail, A. H., 11
Isometric strength building, 48–
49

Jabbar, Karim Abdul, 155
Jones, Ann Hayden, 39, 128

Kim, Han Joo, 22–23
Kinesthetic data: stored in memory, 56; warmup and memory
of, 78
King, Alan, 85
King, Billie Jean, 11; anxiety of,
32, 33; conjecture on background of, 146; dominance by,
125, 127, 128; in doubles play,
107; hating to lose as championship quality in opinion of, 82;
intimidating, 153; and magic
helper of Olga Morozova, 62;
on money, 12; as playing a
"man's game," 150; on playing
out of her brain, 37; Riggs defeated by, 145, 147; risk-taking
by, 152; thinking of tennis as
related to winning in opinion
of, 100
Kodes, Jan: and Nastase gamesmanship, 115–16
Korbut, Olga, 138
Kramer, Jack, 13; and Gonzales'
dominance, 126

Index

Laver, Rod, 12, 13, 159; concentration of, 34, 38; dominance by, 127; kept out of senior play, 4; and lobbing the ball, 105

Learning: in precision, 60–69; use of memory in, 58

Little League sports, 18

Long-term memory, 56–59

Louis, Joe, 39

Losers, 112–35; case study on, 128–33; gamesman as, 113–16; "in" players as, 122–24; self-defeated as, 133–35; submissives as, 124–28

Lutz, Bob, 127, 165

Machiavelli, Nicolo, 113

McKay, Barry, 4

McLaughlin, Donal, 88

McMillan, Frew: magic helper of, 62

Magic: and analytic thought, 64; as form of learning by association, 61, 62; losers and, 125; magic helpers, 62

Maharishi Mahesh Yogi, 88

Meditation, 88–90

Memory: in precision, 55–60

Mental practice: as warmup, 77–79

Metabolism, 45–47; see also Fitness

Mischel, Walter, 82

Mixed doubles, 110–11

Money: individual worth and, 12–13

Mood (transient) depression, 162–63

Moran, Gussie, 126, 132

Morehouse, Lawrence, 92

Morozova, Olga, 163; in doubles play, 108; magic helper of, 62

Motivation, 9–25; accentuation and, 55; of creative people, 75; defined, 9; as essential, 7; influence of, on memory, 57–58; in tennis personality, 82

Motivational distraction: concentration and coping with, 37–40

Motivational readiness: defined, 35

Motives, 10–13; defined, 9; see also Motivation

Mulloy, Gardnar, xii, 4; magic helper of, 62

Muscles: collapse of, 160–61; diet and, 118–22; effects of heat and humidity on, 95, 96; exercise and circulation to, 77–78; sex and, 93, 94; sex differences in, 139; in skill factor, 42–45

Nastase, Ilie, 13; behavior of, 150; chronic exhaustion of, 159; court personality of, 80, 81; distracting, 102; dominance by, 127; in doubles play, 107; gamesmanship by, 115–16; precompetition arousal in, 85

Navratilova, Martina: in doubles play, 108; intimidating, 153

New York Times, The (newspaper), 88

Newcombe, John, 13, 32; precompetition arousal in, 85

Nixon, Richard M., 155

Ocean City International Tournament (1977), 165

Okker, Tom, 13